齐鲁文化经典文库

论语今译

杨伯峻 吴树平 今译
潘富恩 温少霞 英译

山东出版集团
齊魯書社

《齐鲁文化经典文库》

出版说明

齐鲁大地是中华民族主流文化的主要发祥地，数千年来，生长在这里的齐鲁人，用自己的聪明和智慧创造了璀璨的文明。首先是在中华文化的整体框架中地位突出、做出重大贡献的先秦诸子，其中影响尤著者大部分生长于斯；其后历朝历代，几乎都有引领潮流、成就卓著的思想家、文学家、科学家等，他们为中华文化的形成和发展谱写了辉煌的篇章，同时也留下了一大批千古流传、影响深远的文化典籍。将这些记录着他们的思想、积淀着丰富厚重的文化内涵、为一代代中国人所承继的典籍系统地予以整理出版，从而进一步扩大齐鲁文化的影响，提高其在当代人中的认知度，促进中华优秀传统文化的积累、传承和弘扬，无疑具有重要的意义。鉴于此，我们向读者推出了这套"齐鲁文化经典文库"。该书的出版系由山东出版集团组织，具体工作由齐鲁书社负责实施。

通过有关专家论证，确定本"文库"的收录范围是那些由齐鲁籍人士（或有一说为齐鲁籍人士）著述的、已经独立成册、在中华历史文化典籍中堪称经典的著作；对像荀子这样原籍虽非齐鲁，但其主要政治生活是在齐鲁地域、其形成影响的思想和主要著述也产生在这里的个别作家，其经典著作也酌情收录。

收录的作品均采用现代标点本，除小说、戏曲之外，其余作品尽可能加以注释，而对先秦典籍则多数予以今译，以便于读者的阅读和理解。所收部分校注本因问世较早,其中难免存有时代的痕迹,诸如高亨先生的《周易大传今注》,陆侃如、牟世金先生的《文心雕龙译注》等,但这些著作是世人公认的具有权威性的注本,仍需得到我们的尊重。

对经典著述的整理出版绝非一日之功,因此,本"文库"在最初集中推出一批后,未出品种将陆续整理出版,谨此说明。

齐鲁书社

2009 年 3 月

前言

《论语》这一书名,有它特定的含义。根据班固《汉书·艺文志》的记载,“论”是“论纂”的意思,“语”是“语言”的意思。孔子在日常生活和执教过程中,发表过许多言论,他的弟子也有不少言论。“论语”就是把这些言论论纂起来的意思。实际上,《论语》所载,不限于孔子及其弟子的言论,也包括了他们不少的社会实践活动。也就是说,书中既记言,又载行。

《论语》共二十篇,每篇由若干章组成。这些篇章排列的先后,并没有内在的联系,即使前后两章之间,也没有什么关连;而且,书中多次出现重复的章节,有些重复章节字句完全相同。如“巧言令色鲜矣仁”一章,先见于《学而篇》,又见于《阳货篇》。还有的不同章节,只是文字详略不同。如“君子不重”章,《学而篇》比《子罕篇》多出十一字,其他文字相同。另外,还有一些章节意思相同,记载有异。如《宪问篇》说:“不患人之不己知,患其不能也。”《卫灵公篇》又说:“君子病无能焉,不病人之不己知也。”两章意思完全相同。从这些现象可以断定,《论语》一书,不是由一个人编辑的。大多数研究者认为,《论语》是在孔子死后,由孔子弟子和再传弟子在不同时期撰辑而成的。

孔子名丘,字仲尼,鲁国陬邑(今山东曲阜)人。生于鲁襄公二十二年(公元前551年),也有人认为生于鲁襄公二十一年,死于鲁哀公十六年(公元前479年)。据孔子自己所说,他是殷商苗裔。周武王灭了殷商,封殷商的微子启于宋。孔子的先祖孔父嘉是宋国宗室,因为距离宋国始祖已经超过五代,便改为孔氏。孔父嘉的后代防叔畏惧华氏的逼迫出奔到鲁国,防叔生伯夏,伯夏生叔梁纥,叔梁纥生孔子。

孔子幼年丧父,家境中落。年轻时曾管理仓库,看管牛羊。他勤于学习，博学多能。三十多岁时，开始讲学授徒，打破了“学在官府”的传统。鲁定公九年（公元前501年），出任鲁国中都宰，迁升为司空，又官大司寇。五十四岁时，代理宰相三个月。当时，鲁定公和执政的季桓子接受齐国女乐，怠于政事，孔子复兴周礼的抱负难以实现，他便带领弟子周游列国，前后长达十四年。他先后到过卫、陈、曹、宋、郑、蔡、楚等国，都没有受到重用。鲁哀公十一年（公元前484年），季康子以币迎孔子，孔子返回鲁国。这时，孔子已经六十八岁了。返鲁后，他把主要精力投入到教育方面，又致力于整理《诗》、《书》、《易》等古代典籍，删修《春秋》。

孔子所处的春秋时代，是奴隶制向封建制过渡的时期，诸侯兼并，战争频仍，礼崩乐坏。为了变革社会现实，他建立了宽博宏大的思想体系。这一思想体系，主要保存在《论语》一书中。

从《论语》中可以看出，“仁”是孔子思想体系的核心。所谓“仁”，用孔子的话来说就是“爱人”。当然，对“仁”的理解不能过于狭窄，它有广阔的内涵。“克己复礼为仁”，“能行五者（恭、宽、信、敏、惠）于天下为仁”，“己欲立而立人，己欲达而达人”也是“仁”。推己及人的忠恕之道，可以说是“仁”的核心，所以曾子有言：“夫子之道，忠恕而已矣。”“忠恕”与“爱人”是一致的。

从“仁”的主张出发，在政治上，孔子要求实行德政，重视教化，刑罚宽弛，经济上惠民，使民“足食”。为了把德政变为现实，孔子主张举拔贤人。

对待天命的认识，孔子继承了原始宗教的天命观，肯定了天的人格神地位。他承认，他的个人品德，肩负的使命，乃至个人的生死和社会治乱，都离不开天命。所以君子有三畏，“畏天命”居于首位。在他看来，“不知命，无以为君子”。但在天命面前，孔子反对消沉，主张顺应天命，有所作为。孔子一方面相信天命，另一方面又不赞同利用卜筮探求天意，对鬼神也采取敬而远之的态度，既不相信，也不否定。这与传统的观念有所不同。

孔子在长期的教育实践中，提出了许多教育主张。“有教无类”是他收取学生的原则,这就使过去没有资格接受教育的基层平民,得到了受教育的机会。这种思想的形成,与他早年卑微贫困的处境不无关系。孔子教育学生的最终归宿,是让他们出来做官从政。在教育方法上,他主张“学而时习之”,温故知新;提倡因材施教,教育内容因人而异;强调“知之为知之,不知为不知”,老老实实地学习;主张治学先要立人,强调品德的重要性。

孔子的思想在中国历史上影响极大。自汉武帝罢黜百家,独尊儒术以后,确立了孔子思想的至尊地位。他的思想影响渗透到中国历史的每一个领域。今天,不论是研究孔子,还是研究中国历史,都离不开《论语》。它在封建社会被尊崇为经典,是每一个学子的必读之书。我们把它翻译成现代语体文,会给学习《论语》的读者带来一些方便。

杨伯峻以前撰写了《论语译注》,由中华书局出版。又撰写了《白话四书》,内有《论语》译文。这次翻译《论语》,是在杨伯峻的两个译本基础上修订而成。修订工作由吴树平独力完成。

MODERN CHINESE TRANSLATOR'S PREFACE

The name of this book, *Lun Yü* (the Analects of Confucius), has its own particular meaning. According to Ban Gu's the History of the Han Dynasty, the character Lun means editing and Yü means speeches. Confucius made many speeches in everyday life and in the course of his teaching activities, and so did his disciples. Lun Yü thus means edited speeches. As a matter of fact, this book records the speeches made by Confucius and his disciples and also includes their social practice. In other words, the book records both speeches and conduct.

The Analects of Confucius consists of 20 books with a number of chapters in each. There is no internal order in their arrangement and there is even no relationship between the adjacent chapters. Moreover, there are chapters that reappear a number of times. Some of them are completely the same, for example, the chapter of "Honey words and flattering looks seldom speak of human-heartedness" first appears in BOOK I XUE ER, and then reappears in BOOK XVII YANG HUO. Some chapters reappear in different words and length, for example, the chapter of "A superior man, if he is not grave…" first appears in BOOK I XUE ER, but when it reappears in BOOK IX ZI HAN, it is 11 characters longer, whereas the rest of it is the same. Besides, some chapters share the same meaning but they are presented in different forms, for example, the chapter of "I'm not concerned at men's not knowing me, I'm concerned at my own want of ability." in BOOK XIV XIAN WEN and the chapter of "A superior man is distressed by his own want of ability. He is not distressed by other's not knowing him." in BOOK XV WEI LING GONG are of the same meaning. It might therefore be concluded that the Analects of Confucius was not compiled by one person, but was, as most researchers agree, compiled by several of Confucius' disciples and their own disciples, at different times after his death.

Confucius' name is Qiu, his personal name Zhongni. He was born in Zuo County of the state of Lu (today's Qufu County, Shandong Province) in the 22nd year of the reign of Duke Xiang of Lu(551 B. C. , or in the 21st year of this reign, believed by others.) and died in the 16th year of the reign of Duke Ai of Lu(479 B. C.). He said, he was the descendant of the imperial family of Shang Dynasty. After King Wu of Zhou overthrew the Shang Dynasty, Wei Zi, a member of the imperial family of Shang Dynasty, was made the prince of Song. Confucius' ancestor, Kong Fujia, was the imperial clansman of the State of Song. It was from Kong Fujia that the new surname of his family was taken since he was five generations later than the ancestors in the State of Song. Kong Fujia's descendant Fangshu went to the State of Lu to seek refuge from Hua's intrigues. Fangshu gave birth to Boxia, and from him came Shuliang He, the father of Confucius.

When Confucius was very young his father died and so he suffered a fall in his family fortune. As a young man, he made a living by looking after cattle and sheep. He was very diligent in learning and he became very learned and versatile. In his thirties, he began to recruit and lecture disciples, which broke the convention that "education must be monopolized by the government". Confucius took the post of the senior official of Zhongdu in the 9th year of the reign of Duke Ding of Lu (501 B. C.) and was promoted to minister of public affairs and minister of crimes, later. At the age of 54, he acted for the Prime Minister for three months. At that time, Duke Ding of Lu and the governor Ji Huan Zi neglected state affairs and indulged in sensual pleasures. Finding it impossible to realize his ambition—the revival of the Zhou Dynasty's rituals, Confucius set off on 14 years' travels through various states such as Wei, Chen, Cao, Song, Zhen, Cai and Chu, but he was not assigned to a high post in any of these places. In the 11th year of the reign of Duke Ai of Lu (484 B. C.) he returned to Lu and was welcomed and given gifts from Ji Kang Zi. At that time Confucius was over 68 years old. After his return to Lu, he was fully engaged in education and he collated the classics such as the Book of Poetry, the Book of History and the Book of Changes and he revised the Spring and Autumn Annals.

Confucius lived in the Spring and Autumn Period, which was a transition period from slavery to feudalism. Vassals annexed territories from each other, wars broke out frequently and there was a decline in social morality. To reform society, Confucius established a grand system of thinking, which was mainly contained in the Analects of Confucius.

It can be seen in this book that Ren (human-heartedness or perfect virtue) is central in his system of thinking. Ren, in his own words, is "to love people". Ren, of course, should not be understood in too narrow a sense since it suggests a much wider connotation. "To subdue one' s-self and turn to propriety is perfect virtue. " "He who can put five things (gravity, openheartedness, sincerity, earnest and kindness) into practice everywhere under heaven is a man of perfect virtue. " "Desiring to sustain himself, sustains others; desiring to develop himself, develops others" is also Ren. Confucius himself put himself in the place of another and this kind of Zhong (loyalty) and Shu (consideration) could be considered as the core of Ren. Zen Zi said, "The Master's teaching consists of the principle of loyalty and consideraion, and that is all. "Zhong and Shu are consistent with "loving people".

From the viewpoint of Ren, what Confucius advocated on politics were: governing by virtue, emphasis on education, mitigation of severe punishment; and what he advocated on economy were: benefiting people and supplying them with sufficient food. In order to put governing by virtue into practice, he suggested selecting and promoting the talents and virtue.

Regarding the will of Heaven, Confucius inherited the views from those of primitive religion which held Heaven as the Deity. He accepted that his personality, his mission, even his life and death, and the social order were all under control of the will of Heaven. Therefore, there were three things of which a superior man stood in awe, and above all else he stood in awe of the will of Heaven. In his opinion, "he who does not know the will of Heaven cannot be a superior man. "But Confucius opposed submitting to the will of Heaven. Instead, he advocated obedience to the will of Heaven and living with a positive aim. Confucius believed in the will of Heaven, but on the other hand, he also was against divining and advocated a reverent and timid attitude toward the spirits and gods, which he neither believed in nor denied. This differs from the conventional ideas of the time.

In the course of his teaching over a long period, Confucius put forward lots of views on education. In recruiting disciples, he followed the guideline "Education recognizes no castes", which, as a result, provided opportunities for the common people to be educated. These people had no right to get an education in the past. These ideas were largely fostered by the humbleness and poverty that Confucius suffered when he was young. The ultimate goal of his teaching was to prepare students for posts in the government. In respect of the teaching methods, he suggested that "One should learn and review constantly one has learned". He thought that by reviewing old knowledge one gains new knowledge. He proposed that students should be taught according to their aptitude and that teaching material should be student-based. He insisted that "say you know it when you know a thing and admit you do not know it when you do not know a thing"—an honest attitude to learning. He put self-cultivation before study and he emphasized the moral sense.

Confucius' doctrines had great influence on Chinese history. Han Wudi rejected other schools of thoughts but held Confucianism in esteem and so its leading position in Chinese history was established. Its influence was so extensive in China that the Analects of Confucius is indispensable even now, either for studies on Confucius himself or for studies in Chinese history. The Analects of Confucius was worshipped as a classic in the period of the feudal society and every scholar was required to read it. We have translated it into modern Chinese in the hope that it may be of some convenience to those who study it.

This book is a revised version based on Yang Bojun's two versions: Analects of Confucius with Translation and Annotation (published by Zhonghua Publishing House), and A Modern Chinese Version of Four Books, which contains the Analects of Confucius. This modern Chinese edition was revised by Wu Shuping.

英译说明

《论语》是中国人的圣经。

在数千年的历史长河中，孔子思想对中国社会、文化乃至民族心理结构等各方面发生了非常深刻而广泛的影响；而且，孔子思想还跨出了国界，在东亚文化圈中居主导地位，可以说，没有孔子思想，东亚文明便不成其为东亚文明；不仅如此，孔子思想对整个世界的影响也是举世瞩目的，人们已把孔子作为改变世界面貌的思想家之一。孔子思想主要记载在《论语》一书里。孔子思想对中国的影响，主要靠一部《论语》；其对东亚的影响，主要靠一部《论语》；其对世界的影响，还是主要靠一部《论语》。

人们普遍认为，在未来世界文化中，孔子思想将继续扮演一个重要角色。这仍然要靠一部《论语》。

由于《论语》的特殊历史地位，历代都有大批的《论语》研究者和注释者。在古代，最经典的注本是朱熹的《论语集注》；在当代，较权威的注本为杨伯峻的《论语译注》；如今，吴树平又在杨氏译注的基础上加以修订，这就进一步提高了其学术价值。

《论语》的英文全译本自上世纪中叶就出现了；其后，又有多种译本问世。遗憾的是，目前反映当代中国《论语》研究成果的《论语》英译本还不多见。正是为了弥补这个不足，我们以吴树平修订的今译本为根据，将《论语》译成英文，同时兼采国外的《论语》研究成果，参考了 James Legge 的 Confucian Analects，Leonard A. Lyall 的 The Sayings of Confucius 和 Arthur Waley 的 The Analects of Confucius 等译本。

在翻译过程中我们发现，由于文化的差异，孔子思想的许多重要概念，在英语中很难找到对应的词，我们只能以大致相当的词译之，而在其首次出现时于括号中标上汉语拼音；其次，《论语》各篇篇名，不过是摘取每篇开头几个重要字眼来命名的，并无其他意义，故翻译时只能以汉语拼音标之；另外，为了便于理解，我们在必要的地方作了少量注解。特此说明。

本书全部英文稿译出后，承亚洲语言与研究中心联席主席 Colin Mackerras 教授和来自美国 Beloit 大学的复旦大学留学生 Jona Thaw Levitt 先生认真作了审校，谨在此深致谢忱！

译文不足之处，愿受教焉。

ENGLISH TRANSLATOR'S NOTE

The position of the Analects of Confucius in Chinese culture is just like that of the Bible in western culture.

For thousands of years, Confucianism has exerted a farreaching influence on Chinese society, culture and on the Chinese psychology. Its influence has extended abroad and Confucianism has held a leading position in the East Asian Cultural Circles. It might be said that East Asian Civilization would not come into being without Confucianism. What is more, its influence on the whole world is apparent since Confucius is considered as one of the greatest thinkers who have changed the world. Confucian doctrines are mainly recorded in the Analects of Confucius. Its influence on China is maintained by the Analects of Confucius; its influence on East Asia is maintained by the Analects of Confucius; its influence on the world is maintained by the Analects of Confucius, too.

It is generally acknowledged that Confucianism will continue to play an important role in the world culture in the future, and this still would be based on the Analects of Confucius.

Owing to its special historical significance, there have been a large number of researchers and annotators of the Analects of Confucius in different periods. In ancient times, Zhu Xi's the Annotated Analects of Confucius was considered as a classic in annotating the Analects of Confucius, whilst in the modern period Yang Bojun's the Analects of Confucius with Translation and Annotation would be considered more authoritative. Now Wu Shuping has improved its academic value by his revised version based on Yang Bojun's annotations.

The first complete English version of the Analects of Confucius was made in the middle of the last century, after which there were a number of different English versions. It is a pity that there are now few English versions which reflect the results of contemporary researches on the Analects of Confucius in China. Therefore we have done service by once again translating the Analects of Confucius into English. This English version is made from Wu Shuping's revised version, with reference to Confucian Analects by James Legge, the Sayings of Confucius by Leoard A. Lyall and the Analects of Confucius by Arthur Waley.

In the course of translating this book, we have found it difficult to render many important concepts of Confucianism exactly into English because of the cultural differences. Therefore they have been rendered in an approximation of their literal meaning, with Pinyin in place of Chinese characters in the brackets for the terms that appear for the first time. As for the titles of each book in the Analects of Confucius, they are merely a few important Chinese characters in the first sentence of each book. They have no specific meaning. So we just put them into Pinyin. We have made some notes when necessary for further understanding.

We are greatly indebted to Professor Colin Mackerras, codirector of the Key Centre for Asian Languages and Studies, and to Mr. Jona Thaw Levitt, an exchange student from Beloit College in the U. S. A. , and is now at Fudan University. They took the trouble to read through the English manuscript and carefully correct it. They helped us in polishing the language.

Needless to say, there are some inadequacies in this book. Any suggestions or comments are welcome.

目录

CONTENTS

学而篇第一

[原文] **1·1** 子曰:“学而时习之,不亦说乎?有朋自远方来,不亦乐乎?人不知而不愠,不亦君子乎?”

[译文] 孔子说:“学到了知识,并时时复习,不是很愉快吗?有志同道合的人从远方来,不是很快乐吗?人家不了解我,我却不怨恨,不是道德高尚的君子吗?”

The Master said,“Is it not pleasant to learn and to review constantly what one has learned? Is it not delightful to have friends coming from afar? Is he not a superior man, who feels no discontent though others do not know him?”

[原文] **1·2** 有子曰:“其为人也孝弟,而好犯上者,鲜矣;不好犯上,而好作乱者,未之有也。君子务本,本立而道生。孝弟也者,其为仁之本与!”

[译文] 有子说:“他为人孝顺父母,敬爱兄长,却喜欢触犯上级,这种情况是很少的;不喜欢触犯上级,却喜欢反叛作乱,这种情况是没有的。君子致力于根本,根本树立了,道就会由此而生。孝顺父母,敬爱兄长,就是‘仁’的根本吧!”

You Zi① said,“There are few who are filial and fraternal but like to offend against their superiors. There have been none who do not like to offend against their superiors but like to rebel. The superior man works upon the root. When the root is taken, the Way (Dao) naturally grows. Filial piety and fraternal submission!—are they not the root of human heartedness (Ren)?”

［注释］ ① i. e. You Ruo, a disciple of Confucius.

［原文］ **1·3 子曰："巧言令色，鲜矣仁！"**

［译文］ 孔子说："花言巧语，一脸媚色，这种人，'仁'就很少了。"

The Master said, "Honey words and flattering looks seldom speak of human-heartedness."

［原文］ **1·4 曾子曰："吾日三省吾身——为人谋而不忠乎？与朋友交而不信乎？传不习乎？"**

［译文］ 曾子说："我每天多次反躬自问替别人办事，是不是尽心竭力了呢？同朋友交往，是不是诚心实意呢？老师传授我的学业，是不是复习了呢？"

Zeng Zi① said, "I daily examine myself for several times: have I been conscientious in working for others? Have I been sincere in dealings with friends? Have I reviewed what my teacher taught me?"

［注释］ ① A disciple of Confucius.

［原文］ **1·5 子曰："道千乘之国，敬事而信，节用而爱人，使民以时。"**

［译文］ 孔子说："治理拥有一千辆兵车的国家，要严肃认真地处理政事，诚信无欺，节约费用，爱护人民，农闲时役使老百姓。"

The Master said, "To rule a country of a thousand chariots, the ruler should attend strictly to business, keep his promises, economize on expenditure, love the people, and use the labour of the peasantry at the proper seasons."

[原文] **1·6** 子曰："弟子入则孝，出则悌，谨而信，汎爱众而亲仁。行有余力，则以学文。"

[译文] 孔子说："后生小子在父母跟前，便孝顺父母；离开自己住室，便敬爱兄长；说话谨慎诚实可信，博爱大众，亲近有仁德的人。有多余的力量，就去学习文献。"

The Master said, "A youth should be filial at home and respectful to his elders abroad. He should be cautious and truthful. He should love all and cultivate the friendship of the virtuous. When he still has time and energy after having done all these, he should study the cultural heritage."

[原文] **1·7** 子夏曰："贤贤易色；事父母，能竭其力；事君，能致其身；与朋友交，言而有信。虽曰未学，吾必谓之学矣。"

[译文] 子夏说："（对待妻子，）重视品德，不重容貌；侍奉父母，能够竭心尽力；侍奉君王，能够献身；同朋友交往，说话诚实守信。（这种人，）虽说没有学习过，我一定说他是已经学习过了。"

Zixia① said, "If a man honours his wife's virtue and withdraw his mind from her beauty; if he can exert his utmost strength to serve his parents; if he can devote his life to serve his prince; if he speaks sincerely in his dealings with his friends: —such a man, although men say that he has not learned, I will certainly say that he has."

[注释] ① A disciple of Confucius.

[原文] **1·8** 子曰："君子不重，则不威，学则不固。主忠信。无友不如己者。过则勿惮改。"

[译文] 孔子说:“君子不庄重,就没有威望,即使学习,也不会把所学的知识巩固下来。要以忠和信两种品德为主。不要同不如自己的人交朋友。有了过错就不要怕改正。”

The Master said, “A superior man, if he is not grave, he will not get any respect, and his learning will not be sound. He should hold faithfulness and sincerity as first principles. He should not make friends with those who are not as good as him. When he has faults, he must not fear to correct them.”

[原文] **1·9 曾子曰:“慎终追远,民德归厚矣。”**

[译文] 曾子说:“谨慎地对待父母的去世,追念远代的祖宗,(这样做,)百姓的道德风尚就趋于忠厚了。”

Zeng Zi said, “Pay a careful attention to the funeral rites to parents, recall forefathers, then the virtue of the people will resume its proper excellence.”

[原文] **1·10 子禽问于子贡曰:“夫子至于是邦也,必闻其政,求之与? 抑与之与?”子贡曰:“夫子温、良、恭、俭、让以得之。夫子之求之也,其诸异乎人之求之与?”**

[译文] 子禽问子贡说:“先生到了一个国家,一定能了解到那个国家的政治情况,是自己打听来的呢? 还是别人告诉他的呢?”子贡说:“先生是靠温和、善良、严肃、节俭、谦逊而得来的。先生这种获得的方法,不同于别人获得的方法吧?”

Ziqin① asked Zigong②, “When our Master comes to a country, he is sure to learn its government affairs. Does he ask the information himself or is it offered to him?” Zigong replied, “Our

Master is benign, upright, courteous, temperate, and complaisant, and thus he gets the information. Is the Master's way of enquiring not different from that of others?"

[注释] ① i. e. Cheng Kang. Some historians consider him as a disciple of Confucius.

② A disciple of Confucius.

[原文] **1·11 子曰:"父在观其志,父没观其行,三年无改于父之道,可谓孝矣。"**

[译文] 孔子说:"父亲在世时便观察他的志向,父亲去世后便考察他的行为,如果三年不改变父亲的所为,可以说是孝了。"

The Master said,"While a man's father is alive, look at his intentions; when his father is dead, look at his conduct. If for three years he does not alter from the way of his father, he may be called filial."

[原文] **1·12 有子曰:"礼之用,和为贵。先王之道,斯为美,小大由之。有所不行,知和而和,不以礼节之,亦不可行也。"**

[译文] 有子说:"礼的运用,以和谐为可贵。先王治国之道的好处正在这里,不论小事、大事都照这样去做。但也有不能这样做的,只知道要和谐而一味求和谐,不用礼节来节制,也是不可行的。"

You Zi said,"In practising the rules of propriety, it is harmony that is prized. This is what is so precious in the ways of the ancient kings. They followed this principle in things small and great. Yet it is not to be observed in all cases. To know how such harmony should be prized, yet manifest it without regulating it by the rules of propriety, is something which should not be done."

［原文］ 1·13 有子曰:"信近于义,言可复也。恭近于礼,远耻辱也。因不失其亲,亦可宗也。"

［译文］ 有子说:"说话有信用而近于义,说的话就能兑现。态度恭敬而近于礼,就能不遭受耻辱。所依靠的是关系密切的人,也就靠得住了。"

You Zi said, "If promises are made according to righteousness (Yi), words can be fulfilled; if respect is shown according to propriety, shame can be kept at bay. If one relies on intimates, he can be trusted."

［原文］ 1·14 子曰:"君子食无求饱,居无求安,敏于事而慎于言,就有道而正焉,可谓好学也已。"

［译文］ 孔子说:"君子吃饭不求饱腹,居住不求舒适,对工作勤劳敏捷,说话小心谨慎,到有道的人那里去匡正自己,这样可以说是好学了。"

The Master said, "A superior man does not seek satiety in his food nor ease in his dwelling-place. He is earnest in what he is doing and cautious in his speech. He associates with those who possess the Way and thereby he may be rectified. Such a person may indeed be said to love learning."

［原文］ 1·15 子贡曰:"贫而无谄,富而无骄,何如?"子曰:"可也。未若贫而乐,富而好礼者也。"

子贡曰:"《诗》云'如切如磋,如琢如磨',其斯之谓与?"子曰:"赐也,始可与言《诗》已矣,告诸往而知来者。”

[译文] 子贡说:“贫穷却不巴结奉承,富有却不骄傲自大,(这种人)怎么样?”孔子说:“可以了,但还不如贫穷却乐于道,富有而喜好礼的人。”

子贡说:“《诗经》上说:‘像对待骨、角、象牙、玉石一样,先切削,再锉平,然后精雕细刻,进行磨光。’大概就是您说的这个意思吧?”孔子说:“赐啊,现在可以和你讨论《诗经》了。(你能举一反三了,)告诉你过去的事,就能推知未来的事。”

Zigong said, “Poor, but no flatterer; rich, but not proud. What do you think of that?” The master said, “It will do, but better still is the man who, though poor, yet delighting in the Way; or the man who, though rich, loves the rules of propriety.”

Zigong said, “It is said in the Book of Poetry: ‘As you cut and then file, as you carve and then polish.’ The meaning is the same, I suppose, with what you have just said.” The Master said, “Ci[1], with you I can begin to talk about the Book of Poetry. When I told you one point, you know its proper sequence.”

[注释] ① i. e. Zigong.

[原文] **1·16 子曰:“不患人之不己知,患不知人也。”**

[译文] 孔子说:“不怕别人不了解自己,只怕自己不了解别人。”

The Master said, “I do not worry about others not knowing me; what I worry about is that I do not know others.”

为政篇第二

［原文］ **2·1** 子曰："为政以德，譬如北辰居其所而众星共之。"

［译文］ 孔子说："用道德来治理政事，就会像北极星一样，安居在自己的位置上，别的星辰都环绕着它。"

The Master said, "He who rules by means of his virtue is like the north polar star, which remains in its place and all the other stars turn towards it."

［原文］ **2·2** 子曰："《诗》三百，一言以蔽之，曰：'思无邪。'"

［译文］ 孔子说："《诗经》三百篇，用一句话来概括它，就是'思想没有邪念'。"

The Master said, "In the Book of Poetry there are three hundred poems. But the essence of them can be covered in one sentence: 'Have no depraved thoughts.'"

［原文］ **2·3** 子曰："道之以政，齐之以刑，民免而无耻。道之以德，齐之以礼，有耻且格。"

［译文］ 孔子说："用政令来诱导，用刑罚来整治，百姓只是暂时地不犯罪，却没有羞耻之心。用道德来诱导，用礼教来整治，百姓不但有羞耻之心，而且言行都归于正道。"

The Master said, "If the people are guided by law, and kept in order by punishment, they may try to avoid crime, but have no sense of shame. If they are guided by virtue, and kept in order by the rules of propriety, they will have a sense of shame, and moreover will come to be good."

［原文］ **2·4** 子曰："吾十有五而志于学，三十而立，四十而不惑，五十而知天命，六十而耳顺，七十而从心所欲，不逾矩。"

［译文］ 孔子说："我十五岁立志学习，三十岁能自立，四十岁不会被迷惑，五十岁能知天命，六十岁对听到的事情能分辨真假，判明是非，七十岁便随心所欲，不离准则。"

The Master said, "At fifteen I set my heart on learning. At thirty I could stand firm. At fourty I had no doubts. At fifty I knew the Decree of Heaven. At sixty I was already obedient (to this decree). At seventy I could follow the desires of my mind without overstepping the boundaries (of what is right)."

［原文］ **2·5** 孟懿子问孝。子曰："无违。"

樊迟御，子告之曰："孟孙问孝于我，我对曰，无违。"樊迟曰："何谓也？"子曰："生事之以礼，死葬之以礼，祭之以礼。"

［译文］ 孟懿子问孔子怎样才是孝。孔子说："不要违背礼节。"

樊迟替孔子驾车，孔子告诉他说："孟孙问我怎样才是孝，我回答说，不要违背礼节。"樊迟说："这是什么意思？"孔子说："父母活着，按照礼节侍奉他们；死了，按照礼节埋葬他们，按照礼节祭祀他们。"

Meng Yi Zi① asked about filial piety. The Master said, "Never go against ritual."

As Fan Chi[2] was driving him, the Master told him, "Meng asked me about filial piety and I said 'Never go against ritual.'" Fan Chi asked, "What did you mean?" The Master replied, "when one's parents are alive, serve them according to ritual; when they are dead, bury them according to ritual, and sacrifice to them according to ritual."

[注释] ① A young grandee of Lu, whose father sent him to study with Confucius.

② A disciple of Confucius.

[原文] **2·6 孟武伯问孝。子曰:"父母唯其疾之忧。"**

[译文] 孟武伯问孔子什么是孝。孔子说:"要让你的父母只为你的疾病担忧。"

Meng Wu Bo[1] asked what filial piety was. The master said, "The children should not make their parents worry about them except when they are ill."

[注释] ① The son of Meng Yi Zi.

[原文] **2·7 子游问孝。子曰:"今之孝者,是谓能养。至于犬马,皆能有养;不敬,何以别乎?"**

[译文] 子游问什么是孝。孔子说:"现在的所谓'孝',只是说能够养活父母就行了。连狗和马都能够得到饲养,如果对父母不恭敬,供养父母和饲养狗马有什么区别呢?"

Ziyou[1] asked what filial piety was. The Master said, "Filial piety nowadays means merely supporting one's parents. But even dogs and horses can be cared for to that extent. Without the feeling of respect, wherein lies the difference?"

[注释] ① A disciple of Confucius.

[原文] **2·8** 子夏问孝。子曰:“色难。有事,弟子服其劳;有酒食,先生馔,曾是以为孝乎?”

[译文] 子夏询问什么是孝。孔子说:“难在对父母和颜悦色。有事情,年轻人替他操劳;有酒饭,给父兄吃,难道这样就算是孝了吗?”

Zixia asked what filial piety was. The Master said,“The difficulty is with a cheerful countenance all the time. If, when their parents have anything to be done, the children undertake the hard work, and if, when the children have wine and food, they serve their parents first, can this be called filial piety?”

[原文] **2·9** 子曰:“吾与回言终日,不违,如愚。退而省其私,亦足以发,回也不愚。”

[译文] 孔子说:“我与颜回讲话,他整天都不提出任何不同意见,像是愚笨。等他回去自己研究,也能有所发挥,颜回并不愚笨。”

The Master said,“I can talk with Hui① for a whole day without his ever differing from me. He seems to be stupid. But when he is not with me I examine his conduct and find he is able to illustrate my teachings. He is by no means stupid.”

[注释] ① i. e. Yan Yuan, disciple of Confucius.

[原文] **2·10** 子曰:“视其所以,观其所由,察其所安,人焉廋哉? 人焉廋哉?”

[译文] 孔子说:“看他所作所为,观察他走过的道路,了解他安于什么,那么,这个人怎么隐蔽得了呢? 怎么隐蔽得了呢?”

The Master said,“See what a man does, observe the roads

he has followed, examine in what things he rests, how can a man conceal his real self? How can a man conceal his real self?"

[原文] **2·11** 子曰:"温故而知新,可以为师矣。"

[译文] 孔子说:"温习旧的知识,而能有新的体会,便可以做老师了。"

The Master said, "If a man can continually acquire new knowledge when he thinks over the old, he may be a teacher of others."

[原文] **2·12** 子曰:"君子不器。"

[译文] 孔子说:"君子不像器皿一样,只有一种用处。"

The Master said, "The superior man is not like a utensil, which only has one specific usage."

[原文] **2·13** 子贡问君子。子曰:"先行其言而后从之。"

[译文] 子贡问怎样才能做一个君子。孔子说:"先把他心里的话实行了,再说出来。"

Zigong asked how to be a superior man. The Master said, "He acts before he speaks, and afterwards speaks according to his actions."

[原文] **2·14** 子曰:"君子周而不比,小人比而不周。"

[译文] 孔子说:"君子团结而不互相勾结,小人互相勾结而不团结。"

The Master said, "The superior man is broad-minded and not a partisan. The small man is a partisan and not broad-minded."

[原文] **2·15** 子曰:"学而不思则罔,思而不学则殆。"

［译文］　孔子说："读书而不思考，就会迷惘；只是思考而不去读书，就会感到疑惑。"

The Master said, "He who learns without thinking is lost. He who thinks without learning remains puzzled."

［原文］　**2·16**　子曰："攻乎异端，斯害也已。"

［译文］　孔子说："批判不正确的议论，祸害就可以消除了。"

The Master said, "Criticizing those incorrect ideas may eliminate harm."

［原文］　**2·17**　子曰："由，诲女知之乎！知之为知之，不知为不知，是知也。"

［译文］　孔子说："仲由，教给你什么是智慧吧！知道的就说知道，不知道的就说不知道，这就是智慧。"

The Master said, "You①, I shall teach you what wisdom is. When you know a thing, say that you know it; when you do not know a thing, admit that you do not know it. This is wisdom."

［注释］　① i. e. Zilu, disciple of Confucius.

［原文］　**2·18**　子张学干禄。子曰："多闻阙疑，慎言其余，则寡尤；多见阙殆，慎行其余，则寡悔。言寡尤，行寡悔，禄在其中矣。"

［译文］　子张向孔子请教获得官职和俸禄的方法。孔子说："多听些，有怀疑的地方，加以保留。其余有把握的部分，谨慎地说出来，就能减少错误。多看些，有怀疑的地方，加以保留。其余有把握的部分，谨慎地去实行，就可以少后悔。言语错误少，行为后悔少，俸禄就在其中了。"

Zizhang① was learning to seek official post and salary. The Master said, "Hear much, remain silent to whatever you stand in doubt, and speak cautiously of the rest, then you will seldom fall into error. See much, put aside what you are doubtful about, and put the rest cautiously into practice, then you will seldom fall into repentance. If you seldom fall into error in your speech, and seldom fall into repentance in your conduct, you are likely to achieve official post and salary."

[注释] ① A disciple of Confucius.

[原文] **2·19** 哀公问曰:"何为则民服?"孔子对曰:"举直错诸枉,则民服;举枉错诸直,则民不服。"

[译文] 鲁哀公问道:"怎样做才能使百姓顺服呢?"孔子回答说:"把正直的人提拔起来,安排在邪恶的人之上,百姓就顺服了;若是把邪恶的人提拔起来,安排在正直的人之上,百姓就不会顺服。"

The Duke Ai① asked, "What should I do to make the people submit?" The Master replied, "Promote the upright and set them on top of the crooked, then the people will submit. Promote the crooked and set them on top of the upright, then the people will not submit."

[注释] ① Duke of Lu from 494—468, B. C.

[原文] **2·20** 季康子问:"使民敬、忠以劝,如之何?"子曰:"临之以庄,则敬;孝慈,则忠;举善而教不能,则劝。"

[译文] 季康子问道:"要使百姓严肃认真、尽心竭力和互相劝勉,应该怎么办呢?"孔子说:"你对待百姓的事情严肃认真,百姓对待你也会严肃认真;你孝顺父母,慈爱幼小,百姓对你也会尽心竭力;你提拔好人,教育能力弱的人,百姓也会互相劝勉。"

Ji Kang Zi[①] asked how to cause the people to be respectful and loyal, and to urge themselves to virtue. The Master said, "Treat them with dignity, then they will respect you. Show piety to your parents and kindness to your children, then they will be loyal to you. Promote the good and teach the incompetent, then they will seek to be virtuous."

[注释] ① A grandee of Lu.

[原文] **2·21** 或谓孔子曰:"子奚不为政?"子曰:"《书》云:'孝乎惟孝,友于兄弟,施于有政。'是亦为政,奚其为为政?"

[译文] 有人对孔子说:"您为什么不从政?"孔子说:"《尚书》上说:'孝啊,只有孝顺父母,友爱兄弟,把这种风气推广到政治方面。'这就是参与政治了,为什么一定要做官才叫做参与政治呢?"

Someone said to Confucius, "Why are you not engaged in the government?" The Master said, "The Book of History says, 'Filial piety! Be filial to your parents and kind to your brothers. These qualities are displayed in government.' This also is to engage in government. Why is it that only holding office can be said to be in government?"

[原文] **2·22** 子曰:"人而无信,不知其可也。大车无輗,小车无軏,其何以行之哉?"

[译文] 孔子说:"一个人不讲信用,是不可以的。大车子没有固定横木的插销,小车子没有固定横木的插销,靠什么来行进呢?"

The Master said, "I do not know how a man without truthfulness is to get on. It is like a large carriage without the cross bar and a small carriage without the collar-bar. How can they be made to go without them?"

［原文］ **2·23** 子张问："十世可知也？"子曰："殷因于夏礼，所损益，可知也；周因于殷礼，所损益，可知也。其或继周者，虽百世，可知也。"

［译文］ 子张问："今后十代礼仪制度的变革，可以预料吗？"孔子说："殷朝沿袭夏朝的礼仪制度，所废除的和增益的，是能够知道的；周朝沿袭殷朝的礼仪制度，所废除的和增益的，也是能够知道的。假如有人继承了周朝，就是一百代以后，礼仪制度也是可以预料的。"

Zizhang asked whether the ritual ten generations hence could be foretold. Confucius said, "The Yin dynasty followed the system of rituals of the Xia dynasty: what is abandoned or added may be known. The Zhou dynasty followed the system of rituals of the Yin dynasty: what it abandoned or added may be known. If there is one that follows the Zhou dynasty, even one hundred generations hence, we can foretell its system of rituals."

［原文］ **2·24** 子曰："非其鬼而祭之，谄也。见义不为，无勇也。"

［译文］ 孔子说："不是自己祖先的神灵，却去祭祀，这是献媚。看见应该做的事情而不去做，这是没有勇气。"

The Master said, "It is flattery for a man to sacrifice to a spirit which does not belong to him. It is cowardice to see what is right and not to do it."

八佾篇第三

[原文] **3·1** 孔子谓季氏,“八佾舞于庭,是可忍也,孰不可忍也?”

[译文] 孔子谈到季氏,说:“他用六十四人在庭院奏乐舞蹈,(这是天子用的礼乐,)这种事情都能容忍,还有什么事情不能容忍呢?”

The Master talked about the Head of the Ji family①, who had eight rows of eight dancers and singers each② performing in his courtyard,“If this matter can be tolerated, there is nothing it can not be tolerated.”

[注释] ① One of the Three Families that had usurped most of the powers of the Duke of Lu.

② An imperial prerogative.

[原文] **3·2** 三家者以《雍》彻。子曰:“‘相维辟公,天子穆穆。’奚取于三家之堂?”

[译文] 仲孙、叔孙、季孙三家唱着《雍》诗来撤除祭祖的祭品。(这是天子使用的礼仪。)孔子说:“《雍》说:‘助祭的是诸侯,主祭的天子严肃静穆。’在三家祭祖的庙堂上,采取《雍》诗的哪一点意思呢?”

The three families① used the Yong Ode② during the removal of the sacrificial vessels. The Master said, “‘Assisting are the princes; the son of Heaven looks profound and grave.’ What possible application can such words in the Yong Ode have in the hall of the three families?"

[注释] ① i. e. the families of Meng Sun, Shu Sun and Ji Sun.

② An imperial prerogative.

[原文] **3·3** 子曰:"人而不仁,如礼何? 人而不仁,如乐何?"

[译文] 孔子说:"一个人,没有仁德,怎样对待礼仪制度呢? 一个人,没有仁德,怎样对待音乐呢?"

The Master said, "A man without human-heartedness, what has he to do with ritual? A man without human-heartedness, what has he to do with music?"

[原文] **3·4** 林放问礼之本。子曰:"大哉问! 礼,与其奢也,宁俭;丧,与其易也,宁戚。"

[译文] 林放询问礼的根本。孔子说:"你问的真重要啊! 就一般的礼仪说,与其奢侈浪费,宁可朴素节约;就丧礼说,与其仪式周到,宁可哀伤悲恸。"

Lin Fang① asked for the main principles in connection with ritual. The Master said, "An important question indeed! In ritual at large, it is better to be sparing than lavish. In the mourning-rites, it is better to exhibit deep sorrow than to pay minute attention to observances."

[注释] ① A person of Lu.

[原文] **3·5** 子曰:"夷狄之有君,不如诸夏之亡也。"

[译文] 孔子说:"夷狄有君主,(却没有礼仪,)还不如中国没有君主。(虽然没有君主,却有礼仪。)"

The Master said, "The backward races, which even have

their princes, are not as good as China which is without them."

[原文] **3·6** 季氏旅于泰山。子谓冉有曰:"女弗能救与?"对曰:"不能。"子曰:"呜呼!曾谓泰山不如林放乎?"

[译文] 季氏要去祭祀泰山。孔子对冉有说:"你不能阻止吗?"冉有回答说:"不能。"孔子说:"哎呀!难道可以说泰山之神还不如林放懂得礼吗?"

The head of the Ji family was going to sacrifice to Mount Tai①. The Master said to Ran You②, "Cannot you prevent him from doing this?" Ran You answered, "No, I cannot." The Master said, "Alas! Will you say that the spirit of Mount Tai knows less of ritual than Lin Fang?"

[注释] ① To the spirit of Mount Tai, the prince alone had the right to sacrifice.

② i. e. Ran Qiu, disciple of Confucius, who was in the service of the Ji family.

[原文] **3·7** 子曰:"君子无所争。必也射乎!揖让而升,下而饮。其争也君子。"

[译文] 孔子说:"君子没有什么与人相争的事情。(如果有所争,)一定是比箭吧!(射箭时,)互相作揖,然后升堂。(射箭完毕,)走下堂来,互相敬酒。那种竞争是有礼貌的君子之争。"

The Master said, "The superior man has no competition. If he has, he must have it in archery. But even then he bows (to his competitor) and thus goes up to the archeryground. (After the competition), he descends and drinks with his competitor. In his competition, he is still a superior man."

[原文] **3·8** 子夏问曰:“‘巧笑倩兮,美目盼兮,素以为绚兮。’何谓也?”子曰:“绘事后素。”

曰:“礼后乎?”子曰:“起予者商也!始可与言《诗》已矣。”

[译文] 子夏问道:“‘笑容是多么美好啊,眼睛是多么动人啊,用素粉来打扮啊。’这几句诗是什么意思?”孔子说:“先有白色底子,然后才画花。”

子夏说:“礼仪产生在仁义以后吗?”孔子说:“启发我的是卜商啊!现在可以和你讨论《诗经》了。”

Zixia asked, “What is the meaning of the saying, ‘How lovely is her artful smile! Her pretty eyes so black and white! The plain ground for the colours?’ ” The Master said, “The painting comes after the plain groundwork.”

Zixia said, “Ritual then comes after human-heartedness and righteousness? The Master said, “Shang①, it is you who can bring out my meaning! Now I can begin to talk about the Book of Poetry with you.”

[注释] ① Zixia’s personal name.

[原文] **3·9** 子曰:“夏礼,吾能言之,杞不足征也;殷礼,吾能言之,宋不足征也。文献不足故也。足,则吾能征之矣。”

[译文] 孔子说:“夏代的礼,我能说出来,(可是它的后世)杞国不足以作为证据;殷代的礼,我能说出来,(可是它的后世)宋国不足以作为证据。原因在于缺乏历史文件和贤人。如果典籍充足,贤人众多,我就可引以为证了。”

The Master said, "I am able to talk about the ritual of the Xia dynasty, but the state of Qi① cannot bear sufficient witness. I am able to talk about the ritual of the Yin dynasty, but the state of Song② cannot bear sufficient witness. This is because of the lack both of their records and virtuous men. If those are sufficient I can adduce them to prove it."

[注释] ① The people of Qi are descendants of the Xia.

② The people of Song are descendants of the Yin.

[原文] 3·10 子曰:"禘自既灌而往者,吾不欲观之矣。"

[译文] 孔子说:"(鲁国举行天子才能使用的)合祭祖先的盛大祭礼,从第一次献酒以后,我就不想再看了。"

The Master said, "At the great sacrifice, even after the libations have been poured, I have no wish to look on."

[原文] 3·11 或问禘之说。子曰:"不知也。知其说者之于天下也,其如示诸斯乎!"指其掌。

[译文] 有人询问大祭的禘礼。孔子说:"我不知道。知道的人对于治理天下,好像把东西摆在这里一样容易吧!"一面说,一面指着他的手掌。

Someone asked for the meaning of the great sacrificial service. The Master said, "I do not know. He who knew the meaning would find it as easy to govern the empire as to lay things here." With these words, he pointed to his palm.

[原文] 3·12 祭如在,祭神如神在。子曰:"吾不与祭,如

不祭。”

[译文] 孔子祭祀祖先的时候,好像祖先真在那里。祭神的时候,好像神真在那里。孔子说:“我若是不参加祭祀,(让人代祭,)就好像没祭一样。”

Confucius sacrified to the ancestors, as if they were present. He sacrificed to the spirits, as if the spirits were present. The Master said, “If I am not present at the sacrifice, I do not think I sacrifice at all.”

[原文] **3·13** 王孙贾问曰:“‘与其媚于奥,宁媚于灶’,何谓也?”子曰:“不然获罪于天,无所祷也。”

[译文] 王孙贾问道:“‘与其巴结住室西南角的奥神,还不如巴结灶君司命。’这两句话是什么意思?”孔子说:“不对。如果得罪了上天,也就不用祈祷了。”

Wangsun Jia① asked, “What is the meaning of the saying, ‘It is better to pay court to the kitchen-god② than to the god in the south-west corner③?’” The Master said, “It is not true. He who offends against Heaven has none to whom he can pray.”

[注释] ① Minister in the state of Wei.

②③ These two gods both are small gods. The god in the southwest corner is considered more important than the kitchen god, though he has no real power.

[原文] **3·14** 子曰:“周监于二代,郁郁乎文哉! 吾从周。”

[译文] 孔子说:“周朝的礼乐制度借鉴于夏、商两代,它多么丰富多彩呀! 我赞成周朝的礼乐。”

The Master said, “The rituals of the Zhou dynasty are inherited and developed from the two preceding dynasties Xia and Shang. How complete and elegant its rituals are! I follow upon Zhou."

[原文] **3·15 子入太庙,每事问。或曰:“孰谓鄹人之子知礼乎?入太庙,每事问。”子闻之,曰:“是礼也。”**

[译文] 孔子到了周公庙,每件事情都询问。有人说:“谁说大夫的儿子懂得礼啊?到了周公庙,每件事都要询问。”孔子听到了这话,就说:“这正是礼呀。”

When the Master entered the Grand Temple, he asked about everything. Someone said, "Who will say that the son of the villager from Zou① knows the rules of propriety? He has entered the Grand Temple and asks about everything." When the Master heard the remark he said, "This is a rule of propriety."

[注释] ① A village where Confucius's father lived.

[原文] **3·16 子曰:“射不主皮,为力不同科,古之道也。”**

[译文] 孔子说:“(演习礼乐时,)射箭不一定要射穿箭靶子,因为各人的气力不一样,这是古代的规矩。”

The Master said, "In archery it is not piercing the target that counts, since men differ in strength. This is the old way."

[原文] **3·17 子贡欲去告朔之饩羊。子曰:“赐也!尔爱其羊,我爱其礼。”**

[译文] 子贡打算不用鲁国每月初一告祭祖庙的那只活羊。孔子

说:"赐呀! 你爱惜那只羊,我爱惜那种礼。"

Zigong wanted to do away with the offering of a live sheep at the inauguration of each new moon. The Master said, "Ci! You grudge the sheep, I love the ceremony."

[原文] **3·18 子曰:"事君尽礼,人以为谄也。"**

[译文] 孔子说:"服事君主尽到礼节,别人还以为他在献媚讨好。"

The Master said, "He who serves his prince with all due rules of propriety would be thought a flatterer."

[原文] **3·19 定公问:"君使臣,臣事君,如之何?"孔子对曰:"君使臣以礼,臣事君以忠。"**

[译文] 鲁定公问:"君主使用臣子,臣子侍奉君主,应该怎样做?"孔子回答说:"君主应该依照礼使用臣子,臣子侍奉君主应该忠心耿耿。"

The Duke Ding[1] asked how a prince should employ his ministers, and how ministers should serve their prince. The Master replied, "A prince should employ his ministers according to the rules of propriety; ministers should serve their prince with loyalty."

[注释] ① Duke of Lu.

[原文] **3·20 子曰:"《关雎》,乐而不淫,哀而不伤。"**

[译文] 孔子说:"《关雎》这篇诗,快乐而不放荡,悲哀而不过分伤感。"

The Master said, "The poem Guanju is expressive of joy

without being licentious, and of grief not carried to the point of self-injury."

[原文] **3·21** 哀公问社于宰我。宰我对曰:"夏后氏以松,殷人以柏,周人以栗,曰,使民战栗。"子闻之,曰:"成事不说,遂事不谏,既往不咎。"

[译文] 鲁哀公问宰我,做土地神牌位用什么木料。宰我回答说:"夏代用松木,殷代用柏木,周代用栗木,意思是说使百姓战栗。"孔子听到后说:"已经完成的事不用解释了,已经做过的事不用劝阻了,已经过去的事不用追究了。"

The Duke Ai asked Zai Wo① about the altars erected in honour of the God of Earth. Zai Wo replied, "The Xia sovereign used the pine tree; the men of the Yin used the cypress; and the men of the Zhou used the chestnut tree, meaning thereby to cause the people to be in fear and trembling②." When the Master heard it, he said, "Things that are finished with, it is needless to discuss; things that have already taken their course, it is needless to remonstrate about; things that are past, it is needless to blame."

[注释] ① A disciple of Confucius.

② Pun on li a chestnut-tree and li 'to be in fear and trembling'.

[原文] **3·22** 子曰:"管仲之器小哉!"

或曰:"管仲俭乎?"曰:"管氏有三归,官事不摄,焉得俭?"

"然则管仲知礼乎?"曰:"邦君树塞门,管氏亦树塞门。邦君为两君之好,有反坫,管氏亦有反坫。管氏而知礼,孰不知礼?"

[译文] 孔子说："管仲的器量狭小得很呀！"

有人问："管仲节俭吗？"孔子说："管仲收取大量的市租，手下的人员从不兼职，怎么能说是节俭呢？"

"那么管仲懂得礼节吗？"孔子说："国君在门口设立一个阻隔内外视线的照壁，管仲也设立一个照壁。国君为了自己与其他国君的友好，宴会时在堂上设置放空酒杯的反坫，管仲也设置有反坫。如果说管仲懂得礼节，谁还不懂得礼节呢？"

The Master said, "How narrow-minded Guan Zhong① was!"

Someone said, "Was Guan Zhong frugal?" The Master said, "He collected a huge amount of taxes, and his officers performed no double duties. How can he be considered frugal?"

"Then, did Guan Zhong know the rules of propriety?" The Master said, "The prince of a state had a screen to intercept the view at the gates. Guan Zhong had such a screen. The prince of a state had a stand for turned-down cups when meeting other princes. Guan Zhong also had such a stand. If Guan Zhong knows the rules of propriety, who does not know them?"

[注释] ① Prime Minister of the state of Qi.

[原文] **3·23 子语鲁大师乐，曰："乐其可知也：始作，翕如也；从之，纯如也，皦如也，绎如也，以成。"**

[译文] 孔子对鲁国的乐官太师谈论音乐说："音乐是可以通晓的。开始演奏，翕翕地热烈；继续下去，和谐而清晰，乐音绎绎地不绝，直到完成。"

When talking about music with the grand musicmaster of Lu, the Master said, "How to play music can be known. At first each part is in unison. As it proceeds, they should be in harmony, severally distinct and flowing without break, and thus on to the close."

[原文] **3·24 仪封人请见,曰:"君子之至于斯也,吾未尝不得见也。"从者见之。出曰:"二三子何患于丧乎?天下之无道也久矣,天将以夫子为木铎。"**

[译文] 仪地的边防官请求会见孔子,说:"有道德学问的人到了这个地方,我从来没有不和他见面的。"孔子的随行学生带他去见孔子。出来后,(对孔子的学生们)说:"你们这些人为什么担心得不到官职呢?天下黑暗腐败的日子太长久了,上天将要把他老人家做为人民的导师。"

The frontier guardian at Yi asked to be introduced to the Master, saying, "When a superior man has arrived here, I have never failed to see him." The Master's followers presented him. When he came out from the interview, he said, "Why are you distressed by your fall? The empire has long been without the Way. Heaven is going to use your master as the guide to the people."

[原文] **3·25 子谓《韶》:"尽美矣,又尽善也。"谓《武》:"尽美矣,未尽善也。"**

[译文] 孔子谈论(舜时的乐曲)《韶》说:"美妙极了,又非常完善。"谈论到(周武王时的乐曲)《武》说:"美妙极了,还不够完善。"

The Master said of the Shao① that it was perfectly beautiful and also perfectly good. He said of the Wu② that it was perfectly beautiful but not perfectly good.

[注释] ① The music mined the peaceful accession of the legendary Emperor

Shun.

② The music mined the accession by conquest of the Emperor Wu, who ovcrthrcw the Yin dynasty.

［原文］ **3·26** 子曰："居上不宽，为礼不敬，临丧不哀，吾何以观之哉！"

［译文］ 孔子说："处在上层地位不宽宏大量，举行礼仪的时候不恭敬严肃，参加丧事的时候不悲哀，这我怎么能看得下去呢！"

The Master said, "High officers without magnanimity; ceremonies performed without reverence; mourning conducted without grief—how can I bear to see such things?"

里仁篇第四

[原文] **4·1** 子曰:“里仁为美。择不处仁,焉得知?”

[译文] 孔子说:“住的地方要有仁德才好。如果选择的住处没有仁德,怎么能算是聪明呢?”

The Master said, “It is human-heartedness that constitutes the excellence of a neighborhood. How can a man be considered wise if, when he selects a residence, he does not fit on one where human-heartedness prevails?”

[原文] **4·2** 子曰:“不仁者不可以久处约,不可以长处乐。仁者安仁,知者利仁。”

[译文] 孔子说:“不仁德的人不可能长久地处于穷困,也不可能长久地处于安乐。有仁德的人安心实行仁,聪明的人知道仁合乎他的利益而实行仁。”

The Master said, “Those who are without virtue cannot for long endure poverty and hardship, nor can they for long abide prosperity and enjoyment. The virtuous rest in virtue, whereas the wise pursue virtue in the belief that it pays to do so.”

[原文] **4·3** 子曰:“唯仁者能好人,能恶人。”

[译文] 孔子说:“只有仁人才能够(合理地)爱人和恨人。”

The Master said, “Only those with perfect virtue can love and hate people.”

[原文] **4·4** 子曰:"苟志于仁矣,无恶也。"

[译文] 孔子说:"假如立定志向去实行仁德,也就不会做坏事。"

The Master said, "If a man sets his heart on virtue, he will practice nothing evil."

[原文] **4·5** 子曰:"富与贵,是人之所欲也;不以其道得之,不处也。贫与贱,是人之所恶也;不以其道得之,不去也。君子去仁,恶乎成名?君子无终食之间违仁,造次必于是,颠沛必于是。"

[译文] 孔子说:"发财和做官,是人人所盼望的;不用正当的方法去得到它,就不去接受。穷困和下贱,是人人所厌恶的;不用正当的方法去摆脱它,就不摆脱。君子抛弃了仁德,怎样去成就他的声名呢?君子没有一顿饭的时间离开仁德,在仓卒匆忙的时候是这样,在颠沛流离的时候也是这样。"

The Master said, "Wealth and rank are what everyone desires; but if they cannot be obtained in proper way, a superior man will not accept them. Poverty and meanness are what everyone dislikes; but if they cannot be avoided in the proper way, a superior man will not forsake them. If a superior man abandons virtue, how can he fulfil that name? Even for the space of a single meal the superior man does not go against virtue. In moments of haste, he cleaves to it. In seasons of danger, he cleaves to it."

[原文] **4·6** 子曰:"我未见好仁者,恶不仁者。好仁者,无以尚之;恶不仁者,其为仁矣,不使不仁者加乎其身。有能一日用其力于仁矣乎?我未见力不足者。盖有之矣,我未之见也。"

［译文］ 孔子说："我没有见到过喜爱仁德的人和厌恶不仁德的人。喜爱仁德的人，是再好不过了；厌恶不仁德的人，他实行仁德，只是不使不仁德的东西加到自己身上。有没有人能够一天把他的力量用在仁德上呢？我没有见过力量不够的。大概还是有的，只是我没有见到。"

The Master said, "I have never yet seen one who loved virtue, nor one who hated what was not virtuous. He who loved virtue would esteem nothing above it. He who hated what was not virtuous would practise virtue in such a way that what was not virtuous never had a chance to get at him. Is anyone able to apply all his strength to practising virtue for a whole day? I have not seen anyone whose strength is insufficient. There may possibly be such a man, but I have never seen one."

［原文］ **4·7** 子曰："人之过也，各于其党。观过，斯知仁矣。"

［译文］ 孔子说："人的错误，总是与和他同类的人相同的。考察所犯的错误，就可以知道他是什么样的人了。"

The Master said, "Men's faults are characteristic of the class to which they belong. By observing a man's faults, it may be known what kind of person he is."

［原文］ **4·8** 子曰："朝闻道，夕死可矣。"

［译文］ 孔子说："早晨听到真理，晚上死去都可以。"

The Master said, "To hear the Way in the morning and then die at night, that would be all right."

[原文] **4·9** 子曰:“士志于道,而耻恶衣恶食者,未足与议也。”

[译文] 孔子说:“读书人有志于真理,却以穿得不好、吃得不好为耻辱,这种人便不值得同他谈论了。”

The Master said,“A scholar whose heart is set on the truth, but who is still ashamed of poor clothes and bad food, is not worth discussing truth with.”

[原文] **4·10** 子曰:“君子之于天下也,无适也,无莫也,义之与比。”

[译文] 孔子说:“君子对于天下的事情,没有一定要怎样干的模式,也没有一定不要怎样干的模式,怎样干合情合理就怎样干。”

The Master said,“The superior man, in dealing with the world, does not set his mind either for anything, or against anything; what is right he will follow.”

[原文] **4·11** 子曰:“君子怀德,小人怀土;君子怀刑,小人怀惠。”

[译文] 孔子说:“君子念念不忘道德,小人念念不忘田土;君子关心法度,小人关心个人好处。”

The Master said,“The superior man thinks of virtue; the small man thinks of soil. The superior man thinks of laws, the small man thinks of favours which he may receive.”

[原文] **4·12** 子曰:“放于利而行,多怨。”

[译文] 孔子说:“根据个人利益而行动,会招致很多的怨恨。”

The Master said, "He who acts solely for his own advantage will arouse much discontent."

[原文] **4·13** 子曰:"能以礼让为国乎? 何有? 不能以礼让为国,如礼何?"

[译文] 孔子说:"能够用礼让来治理国家吗? 这有什么困难呢? 如果不能用礼让来治理国家,又怎样来对待礼仪呢?"

The Master said, "If a prince is able to govern his kingdom by the rules of propriety, what difficulty will he have? If he cannot do so, what has he to do with the rules of propriety?"

[原文] **4·14** 子曰:"不患无位,患所以立。不患莫己知,求为可知也。"

[译文] 孔子说:"不愁没有职位,只愁没有自立的本领;不怕没有人了解自己,但求有被别人了解的才能。"

The Master said, "I am not concerned that I am not in office. What I am concerned is how I may qualify myself for office. I am not concerned that I am not known. I seek to be worthy to be known."

[原文] **4·15** 子曰:"参乎! 吾道一以贯之。"曾子曰:"唯。"

子出,门人问曰:"何谓也?"曾子曰:"夫子之道,忠恕而已矣。"

[译文] 孔子说:"参呀! 我的学说贯穿着一个基本观念。"曾子说:"是的。"

孔子走出去以后,别的学生问曾子说:"这是什么意思?"

曾子说："他老人家的学说，只是忠和恕罢了。"

The Master said, "Shen①! All my teachings are linked together by one principle." "Quite so," replied Zeng Zi.

When the Master had left the room, the disciples asked, "What did he mean?" Zeng Zi replied, "Our Master's teaching consists of the principle of loyalty (Zhong) and consideration (Shun), and that is all."

［注释］ ① Personal name of Zeng Zi.

［原文］ **4·16 子曰："君子喻于义，小人喻于利。"**

［译文］ 孔子说："君子懂得义，小人懂得利。"

The Master said, "The superior man comprehends righteousness (Yi); the small man comprehends profit (Li)."

［原文］ **4·17 子曰："见贤思齐焉，见不贤而内自省也。"**

［译文］ 孔子说："看见贤人，便应该想向他看齐；看见不贤的人，便应该自我反省有没有同他类似的毛病。"

The Master said, "When we see a man of virtue and talent, we should think of equalling them; when we see a man of a contrary character, we should turn inwards and examine ourselves."

［原文］ **4·18 子曰："事父母几谏，见志不从，又敬不违，劳而不怨。"**

［译文］ 孔子说："侍奉父母，如果他们有不对的地方，应该婉转地劝止。他们不听从，仍然恭敬，不加违抗，虽然忧愁，但不怨恨。"

The Master said, "In serving his parents, a son may gently remonstrate with them when they are wrong. But if he sees that they are not inclined to follow his advice, he should resume an attitude of reverence and not offend them; he may feel worried, but not resentful."

[原文] **4·19 子曰:"父母在,不远游,游必有方。"**

[译文] 孔子说:"父母在世,不出远门。如果要出远门,必须有一定的去处。"

The Master said, "While his parents are alive, the son should not be far away from home. Or if he does so, he must have a fixed place to which he goes."

[原文] **4·20 子曰:"三年无改于父之道,可谓孝矣。"**

[译文] 孔子说:"父亲死后,如果三年不改变父亲之所为,可以说是尽孝了。"

The Master said, "If the son for three years does not alter from the way of his father, he may be called filial."

[原文] **4·21 子曰:"父母之年,不可不知也。一则以喜,一则以惧。"**

[译文] 孔子说:"父母的年龄不能不知道,一方面因为他们高寿而高兴,另一方面又为他们寿高而有所恐惧。"

The Master said, "The age of parents should always be kept in the memory, at once for joy and for fear."

[原文] **4·22 子曰:"古者言之不出,耻躬之不逮也。"**

[译文] 孔子说:"古时候人们不轻易把话说出口,因为他们以说得出而做不到为可耻。"

The Master said,"The ancients did not readily give utterance to their words. Because they would feel disgraceful if their actions did not come up to them."

[原文] 4·23 子曰:"以约失之者鲜矣。"

[译文] 孔子说:"因为对自己节制、约束而发生过失,这种情况是很少的。"

The Master said,"Those who err on the side of strictness are few indeed!"

[原文] 4·24 子曰:"君子欲讷于言而敏于行。"

[译文] 孔子说:"君子言语要迟钝,行动要敏捷。"

The Master said,"The superior man should be slow in words and earnest in deeds."

[原文] 4·25 子曰:"德不孤,必有邻。"

[译文] 孔子说:"有道德的人不会孤单,一定会有人和他做伴。"

The Master said,"A man of virtue will never be left to stand alone, he must have companions."

[原文] 4·26 子游曰:"事君数,斯辱矣;朋友数,斯疏矣。"

[译文] 子游说:"侍奉君主过于烦琐,就会招致侮辱;对待朋友过于亲密,反而会被疏远。"

Ziyou said,"In serving a prince, frequent remonstrances lead to disgrace. Between friends, frequent reproofs lead to estrangement."

公冶长篇第五

[原文] **5·1** 子谓公冶长:“可妻也。虽在缧绁之中,非其罪也。”以其子妻之。

[译文] 孔子谈论公冶长,说:“可以把女儿嫁给他。他虽然曾被关在监狱中,但不是他的罪过。”便把自己的女儿嫁给他。

The Master said of Gongye Chang①, “I may marry my daughter to this man. Although he has been put in prison, he was not guilty of any crime. ” He married his daughter to him.

[注释] ① A disciple of Confucius.

[原文] **5·2** 子谓南容:“邦有道,不废;邦无道,免于刑戮。”以其兄之子妻之。

[译文] 孔子谈论南容,说他:“国家政治清明时,总有官做,不被废弃;国家政治黑暗时,也不致遭受刑罚。”于是把自己哥哥的女儿嫁给他。

The Master said of Nan Rong①, “When the country was well governed, he would not be out of office; and when the country was ill governed, he would avoid punishment. ” He married his elder brother's daughter to him.

[注释] ① A disciple of Confucius.

[原文] **5·3** 子谓子贱:“君子哉若人!鲁无君子者,斯焉取斯?”

[译文] 孔子评论宓子贱,说:“这人是君子呀!假若鲁国没有君

子,这样的人从哪里得到这种好品德呢?”

The Master said of Zijian①,“A superior man indeed is such a man! If there were no superior men in the state of Lu, how could he have acquired this virtue?”

[注释] ① A disciple of Confucius.

[原文] **5·4 子贡问曰:“赐也何如?”子曰:“女,器也。”曰:“何器也?”曰:“瑚琏也。”**

[译文] 子贡问道:“我是一个怎样的人?”孔子说:“你好比是一个器皿。”子贡道:“什么器皿?”孔子道:“宗庙里盛黍稷的瑚琏。”

Zigong asked,“What do you think of me?”The Master said,“You are a utensil.”Zigong further asked,“What sort of utensil?”The Master said,“A fine sacrificial utensil.”

[原文] **5·5 或曰:“雍也仁而不佞。”子曰:“焉用佞?御人以口给,屡憎于人。不知其仁,焉用佞?”**

[译文] 有人说:“冉雍这个人有仁德,却没有口才。”孔子说:“何必要口才呢?强嘴利舌地同人家辩驳,常常被人讨厌。我不知道冉雍是否仁德,但为什么要有口才呢?”

Someone said,“Yong①is virtuous, but he is a poor talker.” The Master said,“What is the good of being a good talker? Those who refute men with tongue-craft often bring about hatred to themselves. I do not know whether he is truely virtuous, but why must he be a good talker?”

[注释] ① i. e. Ran Yong, a disciple of Confucius.

[原文] **5·6 子使漆雕开仕。对曰:“吾斯之未能信。”子说。**

[译文] 孔子叫漆雕开去做官。他回答说:“我对这个还没有信心。”孔子很高兴。

The Master asked Qidiao Kai① to take office. He replied, “I do not have enough confidence for that yet.” The Master was pleased.

[注释] ① A disciple of Confucius.

[原文] **5·7** 子曰:“道不行,乘桴浮于海。从我者,其由与?”子路闻之喜。子曰:“由也好勇过我,无所取材。”

[译文] 孔子说:“我的主张不能实行,只好坐着木筏到海外去,跟随我的恐怕只有仲由吧?”子路听到了很高兴。孔子说:“仲由的勇敢精神超过了我,但不能裁夺事理。”

The Master said, “If my doctrines make no way, I will get upon a raft and float out to sea. I am afraid only You would come with me.” Zilu was glad to hear this. The Master said, “You is fonder of daring than I am. He does not exercise his judgement upon matters.”

[原文] **5·8** 孟武伯问子路仁乎?子曰:“不知也。”又问。子曰:“由也,千乘之国,可使治其赋也,不知其仁也。”

“求也何如?”子曰:“求也,千室之邑,百乘之家,可使为之宰也,不知其仁也。”

“赤也何如?”子曰:“赤也,束带立于朝,可使与宾客言也,不知其仁也。”

[译文] 孟武伯向孔子问子路有没有仁德。孔子说:“不晓得。”他又

问。孔子说:“仲由这个人,如果有一千辆兵车的国家,可以叫他负责兵役和军政的工作。至于他有没有仁德,我却不晓得。”

孟武伯继续问:“冉求这人又怎么样呢?”孔子道:“求啊,千户人口的县,可以叫他当县长;百辆兵车的大夫封地,可以叫他当总管。至于他有没有仁德,我也不晓得。”

“公西赤又怎么样呢?”孔子说:“赤啊,穿着礼服,立于朝廷之中,可以叫他接待外宾,办理交涉。至于他有没有仁德,我也不晓得。”

Meng Wu Bo asked whether Zilu was perfectly virtuous. The Master said, “I do not know.” He asked again, the Master replied, “In a country of a thousand chariots, You might be trusted to manage the military forces, but I do not know whether he is perfectly virtuous.”

“And what do you say of Qiu①?” The Master replied. “In a country of a thousand families, or in a house of a hundred chariots, Qiu might be trusted as governor, but I do not know whether he is perfectly virtuous.”

“What do you say of Chi②?” The Master replied, “In his full dress, standing in a court, Chi might well be charged to converse with the visitors and guests, but I do not know whether he is perfectly virtuous.”

[注释] ① i. e. Ran You.

② i. e. Gongxi Hua, disciple of Confucius.

[原文] **5·9 子谓子贡曰:“女与回也孰愈?”对曰:“赐也何敢望回?回也闻一以知十,赐也闻一以知二。”子曰:“弗如也;吾与女弗如也。”**

[译文] 孔子对子贡说:“你和颜回,哪一个强些?”子贡回答说:

"我怎敢和颜回相比？颜回听到一件事，可以推知十件事；我听到一件事，只能推知两件事。"孔子说："赶不上他。我同意你的话，是赶不上他。"

The Master said to Zigong, "Who is the better, you or Hui?" Zigong replied, "How dare I compare myself with Hui? When hearing one thing, Hui is able to know ten other things; When hearing one thing I can only know two." The Master said, "You are not equal to him. I agree with you. You are not equal to him."

［原文］ **5·10 宰予昼寝。子曰："朽木不可雕也，粪土之墙不可杇也；于予与何诛？"子曰："始吾于人也，听其言而信其行；今吾于人也，听其言而观其行。于予与改是。"**

［译文］ 宰予在白天睡觉。孔子说："腐烂了的木头不可雕刻，粪土似的墙壁粉刷不得；对于宰予不值得责备。"又说："最初我对人家，听到他的话，便相信他的行为；今天，我对人家，听到他的话，却要考察他的行为。从宰予的这件事以后，我改变了态度。"

Zai Yu① slept during the day time. The Master said, "Rotten wood cannot be carved, a wall of dried dung cannot be trowelled. This Yu! What is the use of my scolding him?" The Master went on to say, "Before, I merely listen to what people said and gave them credit for their conduct. Now I not only give ear to what they say, but also keep an eye on what they do, It was my dealings with Yu that brought about this change."

［注释］ ① i. e. Zai Wo, disciple of Confucius.

[原文] **5·11** 子曰:“吾未见刚者。”或对曰:“申枨。”子曰:“枨也欲,焉得刚?”

[译文] 孔子说:“我没见过刚毅不屈的人。”有人回答说:“申枨是这样的人。”孔子说:“申枨欲望太多,哪里能够刚毅不屈?”

The Master said, “I have never yet seen a steadfast man.” Someone replied, “There is Shen Cheng!” The Master said, “Cheng, he has too many desires, how can he be called steadfast?”

[原文] **5·12** 子贡曰:“我不欲人之加诸我也,吾亦欲无加诸人。”子曰:“赐也,非尔所及也。”

[译文] 子贡说:“我不想别人强加于我,我也不想强加于别人。”孔子说:“赐,这不是你所能做到的。”

Zigong said, “What I do not want others to do to me, I also do not want to do to others.” The Master said, “Ci, this is not what you can attain to.”

[原文] **5·13** 子贡曰:“夫子之文章,可得而闻也;夫子之言性与天道,不可得而闻也。”

[译文] 子贡说:“老师关于文献方面的学问,我们听得到;老师关于天性和天道的言论,我们听不到。”

Zigong said, “The Master's teaching about historical records may be heard. But his discourses about man's nature and the way of Heaven cannot be heard.”

[原文] **5·14** 子路有闻,未之能行,唯恐有闻。

[译文] 子路听到某件事,还没有能够去做,便唯恐听到另一件事。

When Zilu heard anything, and had not yet put it into practice, he was only afraid that he would hear something else.

[原文] 5·15 子贡问曰："孔文子何以谓之'文'也?"子曰："敏而好学,不耻下问,是以谓之'文'也。"

[译文] 子贡问道："孔文子凭什么谥号为'文'?"孔子说："他聪敏好学,谦虚下问,不以为耻,所以用'文'字做他的谥号。"

Zigong asked, saying, "Why was Kong Wen Zi conferred the posthumous title of Wen (cultured)?" The Master said, "He was diligent and fond of learning, and he was not ashamed to ask and learn from his inferiors. That is why he has been conferred the posthumous title of Wen."

[原文] 5·16 子谓子产："有君子之道四焉:其行己也恭,其事上也敬,其养民也惠,其使民也义。"

[译文] 孔子评论子产,说他："有四种行为合于君子之道:他自己的行为庄重,他奉事君主恭敬,他养护百姓有恩惠,他役使百姓合乎道理。"

The Master said of Zichan①, "He had four of the virtues of a superior man: in his own conduct, he was courteous; in serving his superiors, he was respectful; in nourishing the people, he was gracious; in ordering the people, he was just."

[注释] ① Minister of the state of Zheng, died 522 B. C.

[原文] 5·17 子曰："晏平仲善与人交,久而敬之。"

[译文] 孔子说："晏平仲善于和别人交朋友,相交越久,越发恭敬别人。"

The Master said, "Yan Ping Zhong① knew well how to make friends with others. The acquaintance might be long, he maintained the same respect to others."

[注释] ① Minister of the state of Qi, famous for his wise counsels, died in 500 B. C.

[原文] **5·18** 子曰:"臧文仲居蔡,山节藻棁,何如其知也?"

[译文] 孔子说:"臧文仲替一种叫蔡的大乌龟盖了一间屋,有雕刻着像山一样的斗拱和画着藻草的梁上短柱,这个人的聪明怎么会这样呢?"

The Master said, "To keep a big tortoise, Zang Wen Zhong① built a hall with the hill-pattern on its pillar tops and the duckweed pattern on its beams②. Of what sort was his wisdom?"

[注释] ① Minister of Lu in the seventh century B. C.

② Such decoration was proper only to the Emperor's ancestral temple and palace.

[原文] **5·19** 子张问曰:"令尹子文三仕为令尹,无喜色;三已之,无愠色。旧令尹之政,必以告新令尹。何如?"子曰:"忠矣。"曰:"仁矣乎?"曰:"未知。焉得仁?"

"崔子弑齐君,陈文子有马十乘,弃而违之。至于他邦,则曰:'犹吾大夫崔子也。'违之。之一邦,则又曰:'犹吾大夫崔子也。'违之。何如?"子曰:"清矣。"曰:"仁矣乎?"曰:"未知。焉得仁?"

[译文] 子张问道:"楚国的令尹子文三次做令尹的官,没有高兴

的颜色；三次被罢免，也没有怨恨的颜色。自己任内的工作，一定告诉下一届的令尹。这个人怎么样?”孔子说：“可算尽忠于国家了。”子张说：“算不算仁呢?”孔子说：“不晓得。这怎么能算是仁呢?”

子张又问：“崔杼杀掉齐庄公，陈文子有可驾十辆车的四十匹马，舍弃不要，离开齐国。到了另一个国家，说道：‘这里的执政者同我们的崔子差不多。’又离开。又到了一国，又说道：‘这里的执政者同我们的崔子差不多。’于是又离开。这个人怎么样?”孔子说：“清白得很。”子张说：“算不算仁呢?”孔子说：“不晓得。这怎么能算是仁呢?”

Zizhang asked, saying, “The minister Ziwen was three times appointed to that position, and manifested no joy in his countenance. Three times he was removed from office, and manifested no displeasure. Each time he made it a point to inform the new minister of the administration of state affairs during his tenure of office. What would you say of him?” The Master said, “He was loyal.” “Was he perfectly virtuous?” “I do not know. How can he be called perfectly virtuous?”

Zizhang proceeded, “When the officer Cui Zi assassinated the sovereign of the State of Qi, Chen Wen Zi①, though he had forty horses, abandoned them and left the country. Coming to another state, he said, ‘The officials here are no better than Cui Zi.’ and left. Coming to the next state, he said, ‘The officials here are no better than Cui Zi.’ and left also. What would you say of him?” The Master said, “He was stainless.” “Was he perfectly virtuous?” “I do not know. How can he be called perfectly virtuous?”

[注释] ① High official of Qi.

[原文] **5·20** 季文子三思而后行。子闻之,曰:“再,斯可矣。”

[译文] 季文子每件事都考虑多次才去行动。孔子听到了,说:“想两次,也就可以了。”

Ji Wen Zi① acted only after thinking thrice. When the Master heard of this, he said, “Twice may do.”

[注释] ① High Official of Lu.

[原文] **5·21** 子曰:“宁武子,邦有道,则知;邦无道,则愚。其知可及也,其愚不可及也。”

[译文] 孔子说:“宁武子在国家政治清明时便聪明;在国家政治黑暗时便装傻。他那种聪明,别人赶得上;那种装傻,别人就赶不上了。”

The Master said, “When the right way prevailed in the country, Ning Wu Zi① showed his wisdom. When the wrong way prevailed in the country, he showed his folly. Others may attain to his wisdom, but they cannot attain to his folly.”

[注释] ① High Official of Wei.

[原文] **5·22** 子在陈,曰:“归与!归与!吾党之小子狂简,斐然成章,不知所以裁之。”

[译文] 孔子在陈国,说:“回去吧!回去吧!家乡的学生们有进取心、有大志,文采也斐然可观,但不知道怎样节制自己。”

When the Master was in the state of Chen, he said, “Let me go back! Let me go back! My students at home are ambitious and they are literarily accomplished, but they do not know how to restrict and shape themselves.”

[原文] **5·23** 子曰:"伯夷、叔齐不念旧恶,怨是用希。"

[译文] 孔子说:"伯夷、叔齐这两兄弟不记旧恨宿怨,别人对他们的怨恨也就很少。"

The Master said, "Boyi and Shuqi① did not keep the wrongs done to them in mind, and hence few resentments directed towards them."

[注释] ① Boyi and Shuqi were sons of the prince of Gu Zhu. Their father left the throne to the younger of the two; but he would not supplant the elder, nor would the elder act against his father's wishes. So they both retired into obscurity. When King Wu overthrew the tyrant Zhou, rather than live under a new dynasty, they starved to death.

[原文] **5·24** 子曰:"孰谓微生高直?或乞醯焉,乞诸其邻而与之。"

[译文] 孔子说:"谁说微生高这个人直爽?有人向他讨点醋,他到邻居那里要来送给那人。"

The Master said, "Who can say that Weisheng Gao is upright? Someone asked some vinegar of him, and he begged it from his neighbour and then gave it him (as from himself)."

[原文] **5·25** 子曰:"巧言、令色、足恭,左丘明耻之,丘亦耻之。匿怨而友其人,左丘明耻之,丘亦耻之。"

[译文] 孔子说:"花言巧语,讨好的脸色,十足的恭顺,这种态度,左丘明认为可耻,我也认为可耻。内心藏着怨恨,表面上却同他要好,这种行为,左丘明认为可耻,我也认为可耻。"

The Master said, "Clever talk, flattering looks and overdone humility—Zuoqiu Ming was ashamed of them. I am also ashamed of them. To conceal resentment against a person and appear friendly with him—Zuoqiu Ming was ashamed of it. I am also ashamed of it."

[原文] **5·26** 颜渊、季路侍。子曰："盍各言尔志？"子路曰："愿车马衣轻裘与朋友共敝之而无憾。"

颜渊曰："愿无伐善，无施劳。"

子路曰："愿闻子之志。"

子曰："老者安之，朋友信之，少者怀之。"

[译文] 颜渊、季路陪侍着孔子。孔子说："何不各人说说自己的志向？"

子路说："愿意把我的车马、衣服、皮裘和朋友共同使用，坏了也没有什么遗憾。"

颜渊说："愿意不夸耀自己的好处，不表白自己的功劳。"

子路向孔子说："希望听到您的志向。"

孔子说："安慰老人，信任朋友，关怀青年。"

Yan Hui and Jilu[①] were standing by his side; the Master said to them, "Why do not you each tell me your wishes?"

Zilu said, "I should like to share chariots and horses, clothes and fur with my friends, and if they wear them out, I would not be displeased."

Yan Hui said, "I should like not to boast of my good qualities, nor to display my meritorious deeds."

Zilu then said, "I should like to hear your wishes."

The Master said, "In dealing with the aged, to be of comfort to them; in dealing with friends, to show them sincerity; in dealing with the young, to cherish them."

[注释] ① i. e. Zilu.

[原文] **5·27** 子曰:"已矣乎,吾未见能见其过而内自讼者也。"

[译文] 孔子说:"算了吧!我没有看见过能够看到自己的错误便在内心自我责备的。"

The Master said, "Alas! I have never seen one who could perceive his own faults and accuse himself inwardly."

[原文] **5·28** 子曰:"十室之邑,必有忠信如丘者焉,不如丘之好学也。"

[译文] 孔子说:"十户人家的地方,一定有像我这样又忠实又守信的人,只是赶不上我爱好学习。"

The Master said, "In a hamlet of ten families. there may be found someone who is quite as loyal and sincere as I am, but not so fond of learning."

雍也篇第六

[原文] **6·1** 子曰:“雍也可使南面。”

[译文] 孔子说:“冉雍这个人,可以让他做长官。”

The Master said,“Yong①, he can be made an official.”

[注释] ① i. e. Ran Yong.

[原文] **6·2** 仲弓问子桑伯子。子曰:“可也简。”仲弓曰:“居敬而行简,以临其民,不亦可乎?居简而行简,无乃大简乎?”子曰:“雍之言然。”

[译文] 仲弓问及子桑伯子这个人。孔子说:“他简单得好。”仲弓道:“若存心是严肃认真的,又执简以驭繁来治理百姓,不也可以吗?若存心是简单的,又以简单行之,不是太简单了吗?”孔子说:“你的话是正确的。”

Zhonggong①asked about Zisang Bozi. The Master said,

“He would do. He does not mind small matters.”

Zhonggong said,“If a man cherishes a reverential feeling for business in himself, though he may be lax in small matters, his governing of the people may be approved. But if he cherishes that easy feeling in himself, and also carries it out in practice, is he not too lax? The Master said,“What Yong says is right.”

[注释] ① i. e. Ran Yong.

[原文] **6·3** 哀公问:“弟子孰为好学?”孔子对曰:“有颜回者好学,不迁怒,不贰过。不幸短命死矣,今也

则亡,未闻好学者也。"

[译文] 鲁哀公问:"你的学生中,哪个好学?"孔子回答说:"有一个叫颜回的人好学,不拿别人出气,也不再犯同样的过失。不幸短命死了,现在再没有这样的人了,再也没听到过好学的人了。"

Duke Ai asked which of the disciples loved learning. The Master replied, "There was Hui. He loved learning. He did not vent his anger upon the innocent, nor did he repeat a fault. Unfortunately he was short-lived and died. Now there is no such a person. I have not yet heard of anyone who loves learning."

[原文] 6·4 子华使于齐,冉子为其母请粟。子曰:"与之釜。"请益。曰:"与之庾。"

冉子与之粟五秉。

子曰:"赤之适齐也,乘肥马,衣轻裘。吾闻之也:君子周急不继富。"

[译文] 子华被派到齐国去做使者,冉有替他母亲向孔子请求小米。孔子说:"给他六斗四升。"

冉有请求增加。孔子说:"再给他二斗四升。"

冉有却给了他八十石。

孔子说:"公西赤到齐国去,坐着由肥马驾的车辆,穿着又轻又暖的皮袍。我听说过:君子雪里送炭,不去锦上添花。"

When Zihua① was sent on a mission to the state of Qi, the disciple Ran You asked for grain for Zihua's mother. The Master said, "Give her a Fu (equals 6.4 Chinese bushels)."

Ran You requested more. The Master said, "Give her a Yu (equals16 Chinese bushels)."

Ran You gave her five Bings (equals 800 Chinese bushels).

The Master said, "When Chi② went to Qi, he had sleek horses attached to his carriage, and wore light furs. I have heard that a superior man helps the needy but does not add to the wealth of the rich."

[注释] ① i. e. Gongxi Hua.

② i. e. Gongxi Hua.

[原文] **6·5 原思为之宰,与之粟九百,辞。子曰:"毋!以与尔邻里乡党乎!"**

[译文] 原思担任孔子家的总管,孔子给他小米九百斗,他不肯接受。孔子说:"不要推辞!有多的就分给你当地的穷人吧!"

When Yuan Si① was made a governor of the Master's family, he was given an allowance of nine hundred measures of grain, but Yuan Si declined them. The Master said, "Do not decline them. May you not give them to your neighbors or villagers?"

[注释] ① A disciple of Confucius.

[原文] **6·6 子谓仲弓,曰:"犁牛之子骍且角,虽欲勿用,山川其舍诸?"**

[译文] 孔子谈到冉雍,说:"耕牛生下的牛犊,长着赤色的毛,端正的角,虽然不想用它作为祭品,山川之神难道会舍弃它吗?"

The Master said of Zhonggong, "The calf of a brindled cow has red fur and fine horns. Although man may not want to use it in sacrifice, would the spirits of the mountains and rivers reject it?"

[原文] **6·7 子曰:"回也,其心三月不违仁,其余则日月至焉而已矣。"**

[译文] 孔子说:"颜回,他的心长久地不离开仁德,别的学生只是

短时期内做到仁罢了。”

The Master said, “Hui is capable of occupying his whole mind for a long time with no thought but that of perfect virtue. Others can do so only in a short time.”

［原文］ **6·8** 季康子问：“仲由可使从政也与？”子曰：“由也果，于从政乎何有？”

曰：“赐也可使从政也与？”曰：“赐也达，于从政乎何有？”

曰：“求也可使从政也与？”曰：“求也艺，于从政乎何有？”

［译文］ 季康子问孔子：“仲由这人，可以使用他治理政事吗？”孔子说：“仲由果敢决断，让他治理政事有什么困难呢？”

又问：“端木赐可以使用他治理政事吗？”孔子说：“端木赐通情达理，让他治理政事有什么困难呢？”

又问：“冉求可以使用他治理政事吗？”孔子说：“冉求多才多艺，让他治理政事有什么困难呢？”

Ji Kang Zi asked, “Is Zhong You[1] fit to be employed in the government? The Master said, “Zhong You is a man of decision, what difficulty would he find in being a government official?”

Ji Kang Zi asked, “Is Ci fit to be employed in the government?” The Master said, “Ci is a man of intelligence, what difficulty would he find in being a government official?”

“Is Qiu fit to be employed in the government?” The Master said, “Qiu is a man of various ability, what difficulty would he find in being a government official?”

［注释］ ① i. e. Zilu.

[原文] **6·9** 季氏使闵子骞为费宰。闵子骞曰:“善为我辞焉!如有复我者,则吾必在汶上矣。”

[译文] 季氏叫闵子骞做费邑的县长。闵子骞对来人说:“好好地替我辞掉吧!若是再来找我的话,那我一定会逃到汶水之北去了。”

The Head of the Ji family sent to ask Min Ziqian① to be governor of Fei County. Min Ziqian said, “Decline the offer for me politely. If anyone comes again to invite me, I shall certainly be obliged to go to the far side of Wen River.”

[注释] ① A disciple of Confucius.

[原文] **6·10** 伯牛有疾,子问之,自牖执其手,曰:“亡之,命矣夫!斯人也而有斯疾也!斯人也而有斯疾也!”

[译文] 伯牛生了病,孔子去探问他,从窗户里握着他的手,说:“难得活了,这是命呀!这样的人竟有这样的病!这样的人竟有这样的病!”

When Boniu① was ill, the Master went to ask after him. He took hold of his hand through the window, and said, “He is dying. It is fate, alas! —Such a man had such a sickness! Such a man had such a sickness!”

[注释] ① A disciple of Confucius.

[原文] **6·11** 子曰:“贤哉,回也!一箪食,一瓢饮,在陋巷,人不堪其忧,回也不改其乐。贤哉,回也!”

[译文] 孔子说:“颜回多么贤明呀!一竹筐饭,一瓜瓢水,住在简陋的巷子里,别人都受不了那种穷苦,颜回却不改变自己的乐

趣。颜回多么贤明呀!”

The Master said,“Virtuous indeed was Hui! With a single bamboo dish of rice, a single gourd of water, and living in a lowly lane, others could not endure such distress, but he did not allow it to affect his joy. Virtuous indeed was Hui!”

[原文] **6·12** 冉求曰:“非不说子之道,力不足也。”子曰:“力不足者,中道而废。今女画。”

[译文] 冉求说:“不是不喜欢您的学说,是我能力不够。”孔子说:“如果能力不够,是走到中途走不动了才停止。现在你是划定了一个界限不肯起步。”

Ran Qiu said,“It is not that I do not like your doctrines. It is just that I do not have enough strength. ”The Master said,“Those who do not have enough strength give up half way, but now you limit yourself and do not even desire to go. ”

[原文] **6·13** 子谓子夏曰:“女为君子儒,无为小人儒。”

[译文] 孔子对子夏说:“你要做个君子式的儒者,不要去做那小人式的儒者。”

The Master said to Zixia,“You should be a scholar after the style of the superior man, and not after the style of the small man. ”

[原文] **6·14** 子游为武城宰。子曰:“女得人焉耳乎?”曰:“有澹台灭明者,行不由径,非公事,未尝至于偃之室也。”

[译文] 子游做武城县长。孔子说:“你在这儿得到什么人才了

吗?”他说:“有一个叫澹台灭明的人,走路不走小道,不是公事,未曾到我屋里来。”

When Ziyou was the governor of Wucheng, the Master said to him, “Have you got good men there?” He answered, “There is Dantai Mieming, who never takes a short cut in walking, and never comes to my house except on public business.”

[原文] **6·15** 子曰:“孟之反不伐,奔而殿,将入门,策其马,曰:‘非敢后也,马不进也。’”

[译文] 孔子说:“孟之反不夸耀自己,打败仗逃跑时殿后掩护,将进城门,便鞭打着马匹,说:‘不是我敢于殿后,是马匹不肯快走。’”

The Master said, “Men Zhifan does not boast himself. He was the last in the flight from enemy. But when his men neared the city-gate, he whipped his horse saying, “It was not that I dared to be last. My horse would not gallop.”

[原文] **6·16** 子曰:“不有祝鮀之佞,而有宋朝之美,难乎免于今之世矣。”

[译文] 孔子说:“假使没有祝鮀的口才,却有宋朝的美丽,在今天的社会里恐怕难得避免祸害了。”

The Master said, “If one only has the beauty of the prince Song Zhao but hasn't the eloquence of Zhu Tuo, it will be difficult for him to avoid injury during these days.”

[原文] **6·17** 子曰:“谁能出不由户?何莫由斯道也?”

[译文] 孔子说:“谁能够走出屋外不从房门经过,为什么没有人

从这条路行走呢?”

The Master said, “Who can go out of a house but by the door? How is it then that no one follow this Way?”

[原文] **6·18 子曰:“质胜文则野,文胜质则史。文质彬彬,然后君子。”**

[译文] 孔子说:“朴实超过文采,就未免粗野;文采超过朴实,又未免虚浮。文采和朴实配合适当,这才是个君子。”

The Master said, “Natural substance prevailing over ornamentation begets roughness; ornamentation prevailing over natural substance begets pedantry; natural substance and ornamentation duly blended make a superior man.”

[原文] **6·19 子曰:“人之生也直,罔之生也幸而免。”**

[译文] 孔子说:“人的生存是靠正直,不正直的人也可以生存,那是他侥幸地免于祸害。”

The Master said, “Man's life depends on uprightness. He who goes on living without it escapes from death merely by good fortune.”

[原文] **6·20 子曰:“知之者不如好之者,好之者不如乐之者。”**

[译文] 孔子说:“对于任何学问和事业,懂得它的人不如喜爱它的人,喜爱它的人又不如以它为乐的人。”

The Master said, “They who love it are better than those who know it, and they who delight in it are better than those who love it.”

[原文]

6·21 子曰:“中人以上,可以语上也;中人以下,不可以语上也。”

[译文]

孔子说:“中等水平以上的人,可以告诉他高深的道理;中等水平以下的人,不可以告诉他高深的道理。”

The Master said,“To those who are above average, the high subjects may be discussed. To those who are below average, the high subjects may not be discussed.”

[原文]

6·22 樊迟问知。子曰:“务民之义,敬鬼神而远之,可谓知矣。”

问仁。曰:“仁者先难而后获,可谓仁矣。”

[译文]

樊迟问怎么样才算聪明。孔子说:“致力于治理百姓所该做的,严肃地对待鬼神,却远离它,可以说是聪明了。”

又问怎么样才叫做有仁德。孔子说:“有仁德的人对艰难的工作抢先干,对获利的事情却退居别人后面,这可算是仁德了。”

Fan Chi asked about wisdom. The Master said,“To devote oneself to the people's just cause, and, while respecting spiritual beings, to keep aloof from them, may be called wisdom.” He asked about perfect virtue. The Master said,“The man of virtue vies for the hardest job and is the last for fame and gain; —this may be called perfect virtue.”

[原文]

6·23 子曰:“知者乐水,仁者乐山。知者动,仁者静。知者乐,仁者寿。”

[译文]

孔子说:“聪明的人乐于水,仁德的人乐于山。聪明的人活跃,仁德的人沉静。聪明的人快乐,仁德的人长寿。"

The Master said,"The wise delight in water; the virtuous delight in mountains. The wise are active; the virtuous are tranquil. The wise are happy; the virtuous are long-lived."

[原文] **6·24 子曰:"齐一变,至于鲁;鲁一变,至于道。"**

[译文] 孔子说:"齐国改革,便达到鲁国的水平;鲁国一改革,便达到先王的大道了。"

A single change could bring Qi to the level of Lu; and a single change could bring Lu to the Way."

[原文] **6·25 子曰:"觚不觚,觚哉! 觚哉!"**

[译文] 孔子说:"觚不像个觚,这也是觚吗! 这也是觚吗!"

The Master said,"A Gu① is not like a Gu. Is it a Gu? Is it a Gu?"

[注释] ① A kind of drinking vessel.

[原文] **6·26 宰我问曰:"仁者,虽告之曰,'井有仁焉',其从之也?"子曰:"何为其然也? 君子可逝也,不可陷也;可欺也,不可罔也。"**

[译文] 宰我问道:"有仁德的人,就是告诉他说'井里掉下一位仁人',是不是就会跟着下去呢?"孔子说:"为什么你要这样做呢? 你如果不喜欢君子,可以叫他远远走开不再回来,却不可以陷害他;可以欺骗他,却不可以愚弄他。"

Zai Wo asked,"A benevolent man, if he was told that there was another benevolent man in the well, will he go in after him?" The Master said,"Why should you do so? If you do not like the superior man, you may let him go away from you and never go back, but you cannot frame him. You may deceive him, but cannot fool him."

[原文] **6·27** 子曰:"君子博学于文,约之以礼,亦可以弗畔矣夫!"

[译文] 孔子说:"君子广泛地学习文献,再用礼节来加以约束,也就不致离经叛道了。"

The Master said, "The superior man, who is widely versed in historical records and keeps himself under the restraint of the rules of propriety, may thus not overstep what is right."

[原文] **6·28** 子见南子,子路不说。夫子矢之曰:"予所否者,天厌之! 天厌之!"

[译文] 孔子去和南子相见,子路不高兴。孔子发誓道:"我假若不对的话,天厌弃我! 天厌弃我!"

The Master had visited Nan Zi①. Zilu was displeased at this. The Master swore, saying, "Wherein I have done amiss, may Heaven reject me! May Heaven reject me!"

[注释] ① The dissolute wife of Duke Ling of Wei.

[原文] **6·29** 子曰:"中庸之为德也,其至矣乎! 民鲜久矣。"

[译文] 孔子说:"中庸这种道德,该是最高的了,大家已是长久的缺乏了。"

The Master said, "Perfect is the virtue Golden Mean! Among the people, it has long been rare."

［原文］

6·30　子贡曰："如有博施于民而能济众，何如？可谓仁乎？"子曰："何事于仁！必也圣乎！尧舜其犹病诸！夫仁者，己欲立而立人，己欲达而达人。能近取譬，可谓仁之方也已。"

［译文］

子贡说："假若有人广泛地给人民好处，又能帮助大家生活得很好，怎么样？可以说是仁德了吗？"孔子说："哪里只是有仁德！一定是圣德了！尧和舜或者都难以做到。仁是什么呢？自己要站得住，同时也使别人站得住；自己要事事行得通，同时也使别人事事行得通。能够推己及人，可以说是实行仁德的方法了。"

Zigong asked, "Suppose there is a man who can extensively confer benefits on the people and assist all, what would you say of him? Might he be called perfectly virtuous?" The Master said, "He is more than a man of perfect virtue. He must be a sage! Even Yao and Shun① would find it hard to do. The man of perfect virtue is one who, desiring to sustain himself, sustains others, and desiring to develop himself, develops others. To be able to draw from one's self a parellel for the treatment of others, that may be called the way to practice virtue."

［注释］

① Two legendary emperors of the golden age.

述而篇第七

［原文］ 7·1 子曰："述而不作，信而好古，窃比于我老彭。"

［译文］ 孔子说："传述而不创作，相信并喜爱古代文化，我私自把自己和老彭相比。"

The Master said, "A transmitter and not an originator, believing in and loving the ancients, I venture to compare myself with Lao Peng."

［原文］ 7·2 子曰："默而识之，学而不厌，诲人不倦，何有于我哉？"

［译文］ 孔子说："把所见所闻默默地记在心里，学习而不满足，教导别人而不厌倦，这些事情我做到了哪些呢？"

The Master said, "To treasure up knowledge in silence, to learn without satiety and to instruct others without weariness—what one of these things have I done?"

［原文］ 7·3 子曰："德之不修，学之不讲，闻义不能徙，不善不能改，是吾忧也。"

［译文］ 孔子说："品德不培养，学问不讲习，知道义的道理却不能按义的要求去做，有缺点不能改正，这是我的忧虑。"

The Master said, "Not to cultivate virtue, not to review what is learned, not to do the righteous though having heard of it, not to rectify what is not good—these things are what I worry about."

[原文] **7·4 子之燕居，申申如也，夭夭如也。**

[译文] 孔子在家闲居，穿戴整齐，和乐而舒展。

When the Master was at home unoccupied, he was neatly dressed, and looked relaxed and cheerful.

[原文] **7·5 子曰："甚矣吾衰也！久矣吾不复梦见周公！"**

[译文] 孔子说："我衰老得多么厉害呀！我好长时间没再梦见周公了！"

The Master said, "How deep is my decay! It is long since I saw the Duke of Zhou① in my dream."

[注释] ① The younger brother of King Wu, the founder of the Zhou dynasty.

[原文] **7·6 子曰："志于道，据于德，依于仁，游于艺。"**

[译文] 孔子说："目标在'道'，根据在'德'，依靠在'仁'，游习于礼、乐、射、御、书、数六艺之中。"

The Master said, "Set your heart on the Truth, hold to virtue, lean upon human-heartedness, and seek relaxation and enjoyment in the six arts.①"

[注释] ① Rites, music, archery, driving of chariot, learning and mathematics.

[原文] **7·7 子曰："自行束修以上，吾未尝无诲焉。"**

[译文] 孔子说："只要是主动地给我一点拜师薄礼，我从没有不教诲的。"

The Master said, "I have never refused instruction to any one, so long as he brought me no better present than a bundle of dried meat."

[原文] **7·8** 子曰:“不愤不启,不悱不发。举一隅不以三隅反,则不复也。”

[译文] 孔子说:“不到他想求明白而感到困难的时候,不去开导他;不到他想说出来而说不明白的时候,不去启发他。教给他东方,他却不能由此推知另外三方,便不再教他了。”

The Master said,“Not until he is eager to know but feels difficulty do I instruct; not until he wants to speak out but fails to express himself do I enlighten. If I present him one corner and he cannot from it infer the other three, I do not continue the lesson.”

[原文] **7·9** 子食于有丧者之侧,未尝饱也。

[译文] 孔子在死了亲属的人旁边吃饭,从不曾吃饱过。

When the Master was eating by the side of a mourner, he never ate his fill.

[原文] **7·10** 子于是日哭,则不歌。

[译文] 孔子在这一天哭泣过,就不再唱歌了。

The Master did not sing on the same day in which he had been weeping.

[原文] **7·11** 子谓颜渊曰:“用之则行,舍之则藏,惟我与尔有是夫!”

子路曰:“子行三军,则谁与?”

子曰:“暴虎冯河,死而无悔者,吾不与也。必也临事而惧,好谋而成者也。”

[译文] 孔子对颜渊说:“用我,就干起来;不用呢,就藏起来。只

有我和你才能这样吧!”

子路问:“您若率领军队,找谁共事?”

孔子说:“赤手空拳去和老虎搏斗,不用船只去渡河,这样死了都不后悔的人,我不和他共事。我要共事的一定是面对工作小心谨慎,讲究谋略而能办成事情的人。”

The Master said to Yan Yuan, “When wanted, then go; When set aside, then hide, —only you and I can attain to this.”

Zilu asked, “If you had command of the army, whom would you like to take with you?”

The Master said, “I would not take such a man who will attack a tiger unarmed, or cross a river without a boat, not caring whether he lived or died. I should take the man who acts with caution and can succeed by strategy.”

[原文] **7·12 子曰:“富而可求也,虽执鞭之士,吾亦为之。如不可求,从吾所好。”**

[译文] 孔子说:“财富如果可以求得,虽然是拿着鞭子做市场的守门卒,我也去干。如果不可以求得,还是干我喜欢的事情。”

The Master said, “If wealth can be obtained according to the Way, even though I should become a groom with a whip in hand to get it, I will do so. If it cannot be obtained according to the Way, then I will follow what I love.”

[原文] **7·13 子之所慎:斋,战,疾。**

[译文] 孔子所小心谨慎的是:斋戒,战争,疾病。

The things which the Master showed his greatest caution about were: fasting, war and sickness.

[原文] **7·14** 子在齐闻《韶》，三月不知肉味，曰：“不图为乐之至于斯也。”

[译文] 孔子在齐国听到《韶》的乐章，很长时间尝不出肉味。

他说：“想不到音乐的美妙竟然达到了这种境界。”

When the Master was in Qi, he heard the Shao, and for three months did not know the taste of meat. He said, “I have not expected that music could reach such perfection as this.”

[原文] **7·15** 冉有曰：“夫子为卫君乎？”子贡曰：“诺，吾将问之。”入，曰：“伯夷、叔齐何人也？”曰：“古之贤人也。”曰：“怨乎？”曰：“求仁而得仁，又何怨？”

出，曰：“夫子不为也。”

[译文] 冉有说：“老师愿意帮助卫君吗？”子贡说：“好吧，我去问问他。”

子贡进到孔子屋里，说：“伯夷、叔齐是什么样的人？”孔子说：“是古代的贤人。”子贡说：“他们互相推让，不肯做国君，都跑到国外，是不是后来又怨悔呢？”孔子说：“他们求仁德而得到了仁德，又怨悔什么呢？”

子贡走出来，答复冉有说：“老师不会帮助卫君。”

Ran You said, “Is our Master will help the prince of Wei?” Zigong said, “I'll ask him.”

He went in and said, “What sort of people were Boyi and Shuqi?” The Master said, “They were ancient worthies.” Zigong said, “Did they have any repentance?” The Master replied, “They sought perfect virtue and they got it. What did they repent of?”

Zigong came out and said, “Our Master will not help him.”

[原文] **7·16** 子曰："饭疏食饮水，曲肱而枕之，乐亦在其中矣。不义而富且贵，于我如浮云。"

[译文] 孔子说："吃粗粮，喝冷水，弯着胳膊做枕头，乐在其中。干不正当的事而得来的富贵，对我来说好像浮云。"

The Master said, "With coarse food to eat, with water to drink, and my bent arm for a pillow, I still have joy in these things. Wealth and honours obtained by unrighteousness are to me as floating clouds."

[原文] **7·17** 子曰："加我数年，五十以学《易》，可以无大过矣。"

[译文] 孔子说："让我多活几年，五十岁时去学习《易》，便可以没有大过错了。"

The Master said, "Add a few more years to my life, I will study the Book of Changes when I reach age fifty. Then I may fairly free from errors."

[原文] **7·18** 子所雅言，《诗》、《书》、执礼，皆雅言也。

[译文] 孔子有用普通话的时候，读《诗》，读《书》，行礼，都用普通话。

The Master used the standard language when reading the Book of Poetry or the Book of History and when practising the ritual acts.

[原文] **7·19** 叶公问孔子于子路，子路不对。子曰："女奚不曰，其为人也，发愤忘食，乐以忘忧，不知老之将至云尔。"

［译文］ 叶公向子路问孔子为人怎么样，子路不回答。孔子对子路说："你为什么不这样说：他的为人，发愤用功，连吃饭也忘了，快乐得忘记了忧愁，不晓得衰老即将到来，如此罢了。"

The Duke of She asked Zilu about Confucius, Zilu did not answer him. The Master said, "Why did you not say: he is simply a man who in his eager pursuit of knowledge forgets to eat, who is so happy that he forgets his sorrow, and does not realize that old age is coming on?"

［原文］ **7·20 子曰："我非生而知之者，好古，敏以求之者也。"**

［译文］ 孔子说："我不是生下来就有知识的人，而是喜欢古代文化，勤快地去追求的人。"

The Master said, "I am not one who was born with innate knowledge. I am simply one who loves ancient culture and who is diligent in seeking it."

［原文］ **7·21 子不语怪、力、乱、神。**

［译文］ 孔子不谈论怪异、勇力、叛乱和鬼神。

The Master never talked of extraordinary things, feats of strength, disorder or spiritual beings.

［原文］ **7·22 子曰："三人行，必有我师焉。择其善者而从之，其不善者而改之。"**

［译文］ 孔子说："三个人同行，其中就一定有我的老师。我选择他善的品德向他学习，并把他的缺点作为借鉴改掉自己的不足。"

The Master said, "When three are walking together, I am sure to find teachers among them. I will select their good qualities and follow them, their bad qualities and avoid them."

[原文] **7·23** 子曰:"天生德于予,桓魋其如予何?"

[译文] 孔子说:"上天赋予我这样的品德,桓魋将把我怎么样?"

The Master said, "Heaven bestowed the virtue on me, What can Huan Tui① do to me?"

[注释] ① An officer of Song. He once tried to kill Confucius.

[原文] **7·24** 子曰:"二三子以我为隐乎?吾无隐乎尔。吾无行而不与二三子者,是丘也。"

[译文] 孔子说:"你们这些学生以为我对你们有所隐瞒吗?我没有隐瞒。我没有什么不可告诉你们的,这是我孔丘的为人。"

The Master said, "My disciples, do you think I conceal things from you? I conceal nothing. I have nothing that I would not show to you, my disciples, —this is my way."

[原文] **7·25** 子以四教:文,行,忠,信。

[译文] 孔子以文、行、忠、信四项内容教育学生。

The four things the Master taught were historical records, conduct, faithfulness and honesty.

[原文] **7·26** 子曰:"圣人,吾不得而见之矣;得见君子者,斯可矣。"

子曰:"善人,吾不得而见之矣;得见有恒者,斯可矣。亡而为有,虚而为盈,约而为泰,难乎有恒矣。”

［译文］ 孔子说：“圣人，我不能看到他了，能看到君子，就可以了。”

孔子说：“善人，我不能看见了，能看见有一定操守的人，就可以了。没有却装作有，空虚却装作充足，穷困却装作富有，这样的人便难于保持一定操守了。”

The Master said, “A sage I will not live to see; enough could I find a man of virtue!”

The Master said, “A good man I will not live to see; enough could I find a man of consistency! Nothing and yet pretending to be something, empty and yet pretending to be full, poor and yet pretending to be rich: —men with such characteristics are difficult to have consistency.”

［原文］ **7·27 子钓而不纲，弋不射宿。**

［译文］ 孔子钓鱼，但不用大鱼网捕鱼；射鸟不射归巢歇宿的鸟。

The Master fished with a hook but not with a net. He shot, but not at roosting birds.

［原文］ **7·28 子曰：“盖有不知而作之者，我无是也。多闻，择其善者而从之；多见而识之；知之次也。”**

［译文］ 孔子说：“大概有一种自己不懂却凭空造作的人，我没有这种毛病。多多地听，选择其中的合理部分加以接受；多多地看，全记在心里。这种求知的方法仅次于生而知之。”

The Master said, “There may be those who can do without knowledge. I am not one of them. To hear much, pick out the good and follow it; to see much, and keep it in memory: this comes next to innate knowledge."

[原文] **7·29** 互乡难与言,童子见,门人惑。子曰:"与其进也,不与其退也,唯何甚? 人絜己以进,与其絜也,不保其往也。"

[译文] 互乡这地方的人难于和他们交谈,一个童子得到孔子的接见,弟子们疑惑不解。孔子说:"我赞成他的进步,不赞成他的退步,何必做得太过分。别人把自己弄得干干净净而来,应该赞成他干净的一面,不要死记住他的过去。"

It is hard to talk with the people of Huxiang. When a lad of that place had an interview with the Master, the disciples wondered. The Master said, "I approve of his progress, and I disapprove of his regression. Why be so severe? If a man purifies himself to come to us, I approve of his purification and will not always keep his past in mind."

[原文] **7·30** 子曰:"仁远乎哉? 我欲仁,斯仁至矣。"

[译文] 孔子说:"仁德距离我们远吗? 我想要做到仁德,仁德就来到了。"

The Master said, "Is virtue indeed far off? I crave for virtue, and Lo! Virtue is at hand!"

[原文] **7·31** 陈司败问:"昭公知礼乎?"孔子曰:"知礼。"

孔子退,揖巫马期而进之,曰:"吾闻君子不党,君子亦党乎? 君取于吴,为同姓,谓之吴孟子。君而知礼,孰不知礼?"

巫马期以告。子曰:"丘也幸,苟有过,人必知之。”

[译文] 陈司败问孔子:“鲁昭公懂不懂礼法?”孔子说:“懂礼法。”

孔子走了出来,陈司败便向巫马期作了个揖,请他走近自己,说:“我听说君子无所偏袒,难道孔子竟偏袒吗?鲁君从吴国娶了位夫人,吴和鲁是同姓国家,不便叫她吴姬,于是叫她吴孟子。鲁君若是懂得礼法,谁不懂得礼法呢?”

巫马期把这话告诉了孔子。孔子说:“我真幸运,假若有错误,别人一定知道。”

Chen Sibai asked whether the duke Zhao① knew propriety. Confucius said,“He knew propriety.”

When Confucius had left, Chen bowed to Wuma Qi② to come forward and said,“I have heard that the superior man is never partial. May the superior man be partial also? The prince married a Wu, of the same surname as himself③, and called her Wu Meng Zi. If the prince knew propriety, who does not know it?”

When Wuma Qi told this to the Master, he said,“I am so lucky! If I have any errors, people are sure to know it!”

[注释] ① A duke of Lu.

② A disciple of Confucius.

③ According to the rules of propriety, a man should not marry a girl of the same surname as himself.

[原文] **7·32** 子与人歌而善,必使反之,而后和之。

[译文] 孔子同别人一道唱歌,别人唱得好,一定请他再唱一遍,然后跟着他唱。

When anyone sang to the Master, and sang well, he would

make him repeat it and join in.

[原文] **7·33** 子曰："文，莫吾犹人也。躬行君子，则吾未之有得。"

[译文] 孔子说："文献知识，大概我同别人差不多。亲身实践，做一个君子，那我还没有做到。"

The Master said, "As for cultural knowledge, perhaps I am equal to other men, but as to carrying out the duties of a superior man in actual life, I have not yet attained."

[原文] **7·34** 子曰："若圣与仁，则吾岂敢？抑为之不厌，诲人不倦，则可谓云尔已矣。"公西华曰："正唯弟子不能学也。"

[译文] 孔子说："讲到圣和仁，我怎么敢当？不过是工作不厌倦，教导别人不疲劳，就是如此罢了。"公西华说："这正是学生们学不到的。"

The Master said, "As to being a sage or a man of perfect virtue, how dare I lay any such claim? It may simply be said of me that I learn without unflagging efforts and teach others without weariness." Gongxi Hua said, "This is just what we disciples cannot learn."

[原文] **7·35** 子疾病，子路请祷。子曰："有诸？"子路对曰："有之。《诔》曰：'祷尔于上下神祇。'"子曰："丘之祷久矣。"

[译文] 孔子病重，子路请求祈祷。孔子说："有这回事吗？"子路回答说："有的。《诔》文说过：'为你在天神地祇前祈祷。'"孔

子说:"我早就祈祷过了。"

When the Master was very ill, Zilu asked leave to pray for him. The Master said, "Is there such a thing?" Zilu answered, "There is. In the Prayers it is said, 'Pray to the spirits in Heaven above and on earth below!'" The Master said, "My praying began long ago!"

[原文] 7·36 子曰:"奢则不孙,俭则固。与其不孙也,宁固。"

[译文] 孔子说:"奢侈就显得骄傲,俭省就显得寒伧。与其骄傲,宁可寒伧。"

The Master said, "Extravagance leads to arrogance; frugality leads to meanness: but it is better to be mean than to be arrogant."

[原文] 7·37 子曰:"君子坦荡荡,小人长戚戚。"

[译文] 孔子说:"君子心地平坦宽广,小人经常局促忧愁。"

The superior man is always calm and at ease, the small man is always fretting.

[原文] 7·38 子温而厉,威而不猛,恭而安。

[译文] 孔子温和而严厉,有威仪而不凶猛,庄严而安详。

The Master was mild, yet dignified; awe-inspiring but kind at heart; respectful but easy.

泰伯篇第八

[原文] **8·1** 子曰:“泰伯,其可谓至德也已矣。三以天下让,民无得而称焉。”

[译文] 孔子说:“泰伯,那可以说是品德极高尚了。屡次把天下让给弟弟,老百姓找不出恰当的词语来称赞他。”

The Master said, “Taibo① may indeed be called a man of highest virtue. Thrice he abdicated the throne to his younger brother. The people could not find proper words to praise him for it.”

[注释] ① Taibo was the eldest son of Gugong Danfu, legendary ancestor of the Zhou sovereigns. The father wished his third son to succeed him, in order that the throne might pass through him to his famous son, afterwards known as king Wen. To facilitate this plan Taibo and his second brother went into voluntary exile.

[原文] **8·2** 子曰:“恭而无礼则劳,慎而无礼则葸,勇而无礼则乱,直而无礼则绞。君子笃于亲,则民兴于仁;故旧不遗,则民不偷。”

[译文] 孔子说:“恭敬而不知礼法就会辛劳,谨慎而不知礼法就会胆小怕事,勇敢而不知礼法就会作乱,心直口快而不知礼法就会尖刻刺人。统治者能用深厚感情对待亲族,老百姓就会走向仁德;统治者不遗弃他的老部下和老朋友,百姓就不致对人冷漠无情。”

The Master said, “Respectfulness, without the rules of propriety, becomes fussiness; caution, without the rules of propriety, becomes timidity; daring, without the rules of propriety, becomes turbulance; straightforwardness, without the rules of propriety, becomes harshness. When the ruler deals generously with his own kinsmen, the people will be incited to human-heartedness. If he does not discard his old friends, the people will not be fickle."

[原文] **8·3** 曾子有疾,召门弟子曰:"启予足,启予手,《诗》云:'战战兢兢,如临深渊,如履薄冰。'而今而后,吾知免夫! 小子!"

[译文] 曾参病了,他把学生召集来说:"看看我的脚,看看我的手,《诗经》上说:'谨慎得战战兢兢,好像面临深渊,好像行走在薄冰上。'从今以后,我知道自己可以免于祸患刑戮了! 学生们!"

When Zeng Zi was sick, he summoned his disciples and said,"Look at my feet, look at my hands. The Book of Poetry says, 'Be apprehensive and cautious, as if on the brink of a deep gulf, as if treading on thin ice.' From now on I know I will escape from all injury, my disciples."

[原文] **8·4** 曾子有疾,孟敬子问之。曾子言曰:"鸟之将死,其鸣也哀;人之将死,其言也善。君子所贵乎道者三:动容貌,斯远暴慢矣;正颜色,斯近信矣;出辞气,斯远鄙倍矣。笾豆之事,则有司存。"

[译文] 曾参病了,孟敬子来探问他。曾子说:"鸟要死了,鸣声是悲哀的;人要死了,说出的话是善意的。在上位的人应重视的仪表态度有三方面:容貌庄严,就可以避免招来粗暴和怠慢;

脸色端正,就接近于诚信;言辞得体,就可以避免鄙陋和错误。至于礼仪的细节,自有主管人员去安排。"

Zeng Zi being sick, Meng Jing Zi① came to ask after him. Zeng Zi said, "When a bird is about to die, its notes are mournful; when a man is about to die, his words are true. There are three principles of conduct which the man of high rank should consider specially important: adopt a solemn attitude and manner to keep from violence and levity; regulate his countenance to keep near to sincerity; utter proper words to avoid coarseness and impropriety. As for temple matters, there are officers in charge mind them."

[注释] ① Head of the Meng clan, high official of Lu.

[原文] **8·5** 曾子曰:"以能问于不能,以多问于寡,有若无,实若虚,犯而不校,昔者吾友尝从事于斯矣。"

[译文] 曾子说:"自己有能力却向没有能力的人请教,自己知识丰富却向知识缺少的人请教,有学问却像没有学问的人一样,满腹知识却像空无所有的人一样,受到触犯而不计较。从前我的一位朋友便曾这样做了。"

Zeng Zi said, "Gifted with ability, and yet consulting those who were not so; possessing much, and yet consulting those who possessed little; having, yet seeming as not to have; full, yet seeming empty; offended against, and yet never contesting: I had once a friend who pursued such conduct."

[原文] **8·6** 曾子曰:"可以托六尺之孤,可以寄百里之命,临大节而不可夺也,君子人与?君子人也。"

[译文] 曾子说:“可以把幼小的孤儿托付给他,可以把方圆百里的国家委托给他,遇到紧要关头能保持着自己的节操,这种人是君子人吗?是君子啊。”

Zeng Zi said,“A man who may be entrusted to a young orphan prince or the fate of the one-hundred-Li state; who in the moment of crisis still holds to his principles—is such a man not a superior man? A superior man indeed!”

[原文] **8·7 曾子曰:“士不可以不弘毅,任重而道远。仁以为己任,不亦重乎?死而后已,不亦远乎?”**

[译文] 曾子说:“读书人不可以不刚强而有毅力,他责任重大,路程遥远。以实现仁德为自己的任务,责任不是很重大吗?到死才停下来,路程不也很遥远吗?”

Zeng Zi said,“The scholar may not have no broad-mind or vigorous endurance. His burden is heavy and his road is long. To practise virtue is the burden he takes upon him, is it not heavy? Only with death does his road stop, is it not long?”

[原文] **8·8 子曰:“兴于《诗》,立于礼,成于乐。”**

[译文] 孔子说:“(人的修养)开始于学《诗》,自立于学礼,完成于学乐。”

The Master said,“By the Book of Poetry a man is first incited; in the rules of propriety he takes his stand; and finally by music he is perfected.”

[原文] **8·9 子曰:“民可使由之,不可使知之。”**

[译文] 孔子说:“百姓可以使他们照着指点的道路去走,不可以

使他们知道那是为什么。”

The Master said, “The people may be made to follow our will, but they may not be made to understand it.”

[原文] **8·10 子曰：“好勇疾贫，乱也。人而不仁，疾之已甚，乱也。”**

[译文] 孔子说：“喜好勇力而又厌恶贫穷，就会作乱。对于不仁的人痛恨太过分，也会出乱子。”

The Master said, “The man who is fond of daring and is inflamed with poverty, may proceed to insubordination. The man who is not virtuous and is deeply ill-treated, will turn to insubordination too.”

[原文] **8·11 子曰：“如有周公之才之美，使骄且吝，其余不足观也已。”**

[译文] 孔子说：“假如有周公那样美好的才能，如果他骄傲而吝啬，别的方面也就不值一顾了。”

The Master said, “Though a man has gifts as glorious as those of the Duke of Zhou, if he is arrogant and mean, all the rest is worthless of even one glance.”

[原文] **8·12 子曰：“三年学，不至于谷，不易得也。”**

[译文] 孔子说：“读书三年，无意于做官得俸禄，这种人是难得的。”

The Master said, “It is hard to find a man who has studied for three years without thought of emolument.”

［原文］

8·13 子曰："笃信好学，守死善道。危邦不入，乱邦不居。天下有道则见，无道则隐。邦有道，贫且贱焉，耻也；邦无道，富且贵焉，耻也。"

［译文］

孔子说："坚定地相信道，努力学习它，誓死保卫，使它完善。不进入危险的国家，不居住混乱的国家。天下清平就出来做官，腐朽黑暗就隐居。政治清明，自己贫贱，是耻辱；政治黑暗，自己富贵，也是耻辱。"

The Master said, "Show unwaving faith in the Way, study it hard and be ready to die in defending and perfecting it. Do not enter a tottering state, nor stay in a disorganized one. When the Way prevails in the world, come out and take office; when it does not prevail, keep concealed. When the Way prevails in the state, count it a disgrace to be needy and lowly; When the Way does not prevail in the state, then count it a disgrace to be rich and honoured."

［原文］

8·14 子曰："不在其位，不谋其政。"

［译文］

孔子说："不在那个职位，就不考虑那方面的工作。"

The Master said, "He who holds no rank in a state discusses no policies."

［原文］

8·15 子曰："师挚之始，《关雎》之乱，洋洋乎盈耳哉！"

［译文］

孔子说："当太师挚开始演奏的时候，当演奏完《关雎》的时候，悠扬的乐声充耳呀！"

The Master said, "From the music master Zhi began to play till the final strains of Guan Ju, what melodious music filled my ears!"

[原文] **8·16** 子曰:"狂而不直,侗而不愿,悾悾而不信,吾不知之矣。"

[译文] 孔子说:"狂妄而不直率,幼稚而不朴实,无知而不讲信用,我无法理解这种人。"

The Master said,"Ardent, but not upright; shallow, but not simple; dull, but not truthful—such persons I really do not understand."

[原文] **8·17** 子曰:"学如不及,犹恐失之。"

[译文] 孔子说:"做学问好像追逐什么,生怕追不上;追上了,又生怕丢掉了。"

The Master said,"Learn as if you were following something to which you can never catch up, as if you were in fear of losing what you have got."

[原文] **8·18** 子曰:"巍巍乎,舜、禹之有天下也而不与焉!"

[译文] 孔子说:"舜和禹真是崇高啊! 拥有天下而不为自己。"

The Master said,"Sublime indeed were Shun and Yu! They held possession of the whole world, but did nothing for themselves."

[原文] **8·19** 子曰:"大哉尧之为君也! 巍巍乎! 唯天为大,唯尧则之。荡荡乎,民无能名焉。巍巍乎其有成功也,焕乎其有文章!"

［译文］ 孔子说："尧作为国君真伟大啊！崇高啊！只有天最高大，唯独尧能够效法天。他的恩惠广博无边，老百姓不知道怎样去称赞他。他的功业真是崇高啊！他的礼仪制度也太美好了！"

The Master said, "How great was Yao as a sovereign! How sublime! Heaven alone is great; Yao alone corresponded to it. Boundless! The people could find no proper words to praise him. Sublime were his achievements! Glorious the regulations he instituted!"

［原文］ **8·20 舜有臣五人而天下治。武王曰："予有乱臣十人。"孔子曰："才难，不其然乎？唐虞之际，于斯为盛。有妇人焉，九人而已。三分天下有其二，以服事殷。周之德，其可谓至德也已矣。"**

［译文］ 舜有五位贤臣，便天下太平。武王说："我有十位能治理天下的臣子。"孔子说："人才不易得。不是这样吗？唐尧虞舜之际，周武王说那话的时候，人才最兴盛。那十人中还有一位妇女，实际上只是九人。周文王得了天下的三分之二，仍然向商纣称臣，周朝的道德，可以说是至高无上了。"

Shun had five ministers, and the empire was well governed. King Wu said, "I have ten able ministers." Confucius said, "It is difficult to find the talents. Is that not true? Only the times of Tang Yao and Yu Shun and the time of King Wu were rich in talents. There was a woman among King Wu's ten talents. So there were but nine talents in all. King Wu possessed two of the three parts of the world, and with these he served the dynasty of Yin. The utmost virtue was the virtue of Zhou!"

[原文] **8·21** 子曰:“禹,吾无间然矣。菲饮食而致孝乎鬼神,恶衣服而致美乎黻冕,卑宫室而尽力乎沟洫。禹,吾无间然矣。”

[译文] 孔子说:“禹,我对他没有意见了。他吃得很差,却对鬼神祭祀很丰盛;穿得很坏,却把祭祀的衣冠做得极华美;住得很简陋,却把力量完全用于沟渠水利。禹,我对他没有意见了。”

The Master said, “I find no flaw in Yu. He used himself coarse food and drink, but he displayed the utmost devotion in his offerings to the spirits and divinities. His common wear was poor, but he displayed the utmost elegance in his sacrificial cap and apron. He lived in a humble house, but expended all his strength on draining and ditching. In him I can find no flaw.”

子罕篇第九

[原文] **9·1　子罕言利与命与仁。**

[译文] 孔子很少谈到功利、命运和仁德。

The Master seldom spoke of profit or fate or human-heartedness.

[原文] **9·2　达巷党人曰："大哉孔子！博学而无所成名。"子闻之，谓门弟子曰："吾何执？执御乎？执射乎？吾执御矣。"**

[译文] 达巷党人说："孔子真伟大！学问广博，可惜没有足以树立名声的专长。"孔子听了这话，就对学生们说："我干什么呢？赶马车吗？做射箭手吗？我赶马车好了。"

A man of Daxiang said,"Great indeed is the Master Kong! His learning is extensive, and yet he has no speciality to render his name famous."When the Master heard this he said to his disciples,"What shall I take up? Shall I take up chariotdriving? Or shall I take up archery? I think I will take up chariot-driving!"

[原文] **9·3　子曰："麻冕，礼也；今也纯，俭，吾从众。拜下，礼也；今拜乎上，泰也。虽违众，吾从下。"**

[译文] 孔子说："用麻织礼帽，合乎传统的礼仪；今天大家都用黑丝，俭省，我赞成大家的做法。臣子朝见君主，先在堂下磕头，合乎传统的礼仪。现在升堂后磕头，是倨傲的表现。虽然与众不同，我仍然要先在堂下磕头。"

The Master said, "A linen cap is prescribed by the rules of ceremony, but now a silk one is worn. It is economical, and I follow the general practice. To bow below the hall is prescribed by the rules of ceremony, but now it is done after ascending the hall. This is presumptuous. I still bow below the hall, though to do so is contrary to the general practice."

[原文] **9·4 子绝四:毋意,毋必,毋固,毋我。**

[译文] 孔子没有四种毛病:不凭空揣测,不绝对肯定,不拘泥固执,不唯我独是。

From four things the Master was entirely free. He made no arbitrary conjectures. He was never over-positive, never obstinate, never egotistic.

[原文] **9·5 子畏于匡,曰:"文王既没,文不在兹乎?天之将丧斯文也,后死者不得与于斯文也;天之未丧斯文也,匡人其如予何?"**

[译文] 孔子被匡地的群众所拘禁,便说:"周文王死了以后,一切文化遗产不都在我这里吗?天若是要消灭这些文化,那我也不会掌握这些文化了;天若是不想消灭这些文化,那匡人将把我怎么样呢?"

When the Master was trapped in Kuang, he said, "Since the death of King Wen, was not all ancient culture (Wen) lodged here in me? If Heaven had wished to let such culture perish, later generations (like myself) would not possess it. But since Heaven has not wished to let such culture perish, what can the people of Kuang do to me?"

[原文] **9·6** 太宰问于子贡曰："夫子圣者与？何其多能也？"子贡曰："固天纵之将圣，又多能也。"

子闻之，曰："太宰知我乎？吾少也贱，故多能鄙事。君子多乎哉？不多也。"

[译文] 太宰问子贡说："孔老夫子是圣人吗？为什么这样多才多艺呢？"子贡说："这本是上天让他成为圣人，又使他多才多艺。"

孔子听到了，便说："太宰了解我吗？我小时候穷苦，所以学会了不少鄙贱的技艺。君子会有这么多的技巧吗？是不会有很多的。"

A high minister asked Zigong, "Is your Master a sage? Why does he has various ability?" Zigong said, "Certainly Heaven intended him to become a sage and have various ability."

When the Master heard it, he said, "Does the minister know me? When I was young I was in humble circumstances. That is why I learned many a humble trade. But does a superior man have such variety of ability? No, he has few."

[原文] **9·7** 牢曰："子云：'吾不试，故艺。'"

[译文] 琴牢说："孔子说过：'我不曾被国家所用，所以学得一些技艺。'"

Lao said, "The Master said, 'Having no official employment, I acquired many arts.'"

[原文] **9·8** 子曰："吾有知乎哉？无知也。有鄙夫问于我，空空如也。我叩其两端而竭焉。"

[译文] 孔子说："我有知识吗？没有啊。有一个庄稼汉问我，我

一点也不知道。我从他那个问题的始末去盘问,得到启发,然后尽量地回答他。"

The Master said,"Am I indeed possessed of knowledge? No! But if a simple peasant asked me a question, I am ready to thrash the matter out from one end to the other and exhaust it and then tell him as much as possible."

[原文] **9·9 子曰:"凤鸟不至,河不出图,吾已矣夫!"**

[译文] 孔子说:"凤凰不飞来了,黄河也没有图画出来了,我这一生完了!"

The Master said,"The phoenix does not come, the Yellow River gives forth no chart①. It is all over with me."

[注释] ① The arrival of this magical bird and the sudden revelation of a magical chart were present that heralded the rise of a Saviour Sage.

[原文] **9·10 子见齐衰者、冕衣裳者与瞽者,见之,虽少,必作;过之,必趋。**

[译文] 孔子看见穿丧服的人、戴礼帽穿礼服的人和瞎了眼睛的人,相见的时候,他们虽然年轻,孔子一定站起来;走过的时候,一定快走几步。

When the Master saw a person in a mourning dress, or in robes of state, or a blind person, he would always rise up, though they were younger than himself; and if he was passing by them, he would always quicken his steps. ①

[注释] ① A sign of respect.

[原文] **9·11 颜渊喟然叹曰:"仰之弥高,钻之弥坚。瞻之在前,忽焉在后。夫子循循然善诱人,博我以**

文，约我以礼，欲罢不能。既竭吾才，如有所立卓尔。虽欲从之，末由也已。”

［译文］ 颜渊长长地感叹说：“老师之道，抬头仰望，越望越觉得高；钻研着，越钻研越觉得深。看它在前面，忽然又到后面去了。老师善于有步骤地诱导我们，用各种文献丰富我们的知识，用礼法约束我们的行为，使我们想停止学习都不可能。我已经用尽我的才能，像是见到了它高高地矗立在面前，我虽然想要追随上去，却没有前进的路径了。”

Yan Yuan said with a deep sigh, “The more I look up to the Master's doctrine, the higher it soars. The deeper I bore down into it, the harder it becomes. I see it before me, and suddenly it seemed to be behind. The Master skillfully leads me on step by step. He has broadened me with culture and restrained me with the rules of propriety. When I want to stop learning, I cannot do so. Having exerted all my ability, there seems something to stand right up before me; but though I long to follow and reach it, I can find no way to do so.”

［原文］ **9·12** 子疾病，子路使门人为臣。病间，曰：“久矣哉，由之行诈也！无臣而为有臣。吾谁欺？欺天乎！且予与其死于臣之手也，无宁死于二三子之手乎！且予纵不得大葬，予死于道路乎！”

［译文］ 孔子病得厉害，子路便让孔子的学生做家臣为孔子准备后事。过了一段时间，孔子的病渐渐好了，便说：“仲由干这种欺假勾当太长久了！没有家臣而装作有家臣。我欺骗谁呢？欺骗上天吗？我与其死在家臣的手里，宁肯死在你们学生的手里。我纵不能热热闹闹地办理丧葬，难道会死在路上吗？”

When the Master was very ill, Zilu had some disciples to act as retainers to prepare for funeral affairs. During a better spell the Master said, "Long has the conduct of Zhong You been deceitful! By pretending to have retainers when I have none, whom do I deceive? Do I deceive Heaven? Moreover, is it not better to die in the hands of you disciples than to die in the hands of retainers? And if I may not have a grand burial, shall I die by the roadside?"

[原文] **9·13** 子贡曰:"有美玉于斯,韫椟而藏诸?求善贾而沽诸?"子曰:"沽之哉!沽之哉!我待贾者也。"

[译文] 子贡说:"这里有一块美玉,把它放在柜子里藏起来呢?还是找一个识货的人卖掉呢?"孔子说:"卖掉,卖掉!我在等待识货的人。"

Zigong said, "Suppose there was a beautiful jade here, should I hide it away in a case, or seek a good price and sell it?" The Master said, "Sell it! Sell it! I am waiting for a man who really appreciates it."

[原文] **9·14** 子欲居九夷。或曰:"陋,如之何?"子曰:"君子居之,何陋之有?"

[译文] 孔子想搬到九夷去住。有人说:"那地方非常简陋,怎么行?"孔子说:"有君子去住,有什么简陋呢?"

The Master wanted to go and live among the nine wild tribes of the east. Someone said, "That place is very poor. How can you do such a thing?" The Master said, "If a superior man lived there, what poverty would there be?"

[原文] **9·15** 子曰:"吾自卫反鲁,然后乐正,《雅》《颂》各得其所。"

[译文] 孔子说:"我从卫国回到鲁国,然后《诗》的乐章得到订正,《雅》归《雅》,《颂》归《颂》,各有适当的地方。"

The Master said, "Only after I came back from Wei to Lu, was the music reformed and were the pieces in the Imperial Songs (Ya) and Praise Songs (Song) properly sorted and given their proper places."

[原文] **9·16** 子曰:"出则事公卿,入则事父兄,丧事不敢不勉,不为酒困,何有于我哉?"

[译文] 孔子说:"出外便服事公卿,入门便服事父兄,有丧事不敢不竭尽其力,不被酒所困扰,我做到了哪些呢?"

The Master said, "Abroad, to serve the high officers; at home, to serve one's father and brothers; to do the utmost in the funeral and not to be overcome with wine—what one of these things do I attain to?"

[原文] **9·17** 子在川上,曰:"逝者如斯夫! 不舍昼夜。"

[译文] 孔子在河边,说:"一去不返的光阴如同这河水啊,日日夜夜不停地流去。"

Standing by a stream, the Master said, "Time passes on just like the flowing water in the river, not ceasing day or night!"

[原文] **9·18** 子曰:"吾未见好德如好色者也。"

[译文] 孔子说:“我没有看见过喜爱道德好像喜爱美色一样的人。”

The Master said,“I have not seen one who loves virtue as he loves women.”

[原文] **9·19 子曰:“譬如为山,未成一篑,止,吾止也。譬如平地,虽覆一篑,进,吾往也。”**

[译文] 孔子说:“好比堆土成山,只差一筐土没有成山,便停止了,这是我自己停止的。又好比在平地上堆土成山,即使刚刚倒下一筐土,仍要努力前进,那也是我自己前进。”

The Master said,“As in making a mound, if I stop when one more basket of earth would end it, it is I that stop. As in levelling ground, if I go on after throwing down only one basket of earth, it is I that proceed.”

[原文] **9·20 子曰:“语之而不惰者,其回也与!”**

[译文] 孔子说:“听我说话始终不懈怠的,大概只颜回一个人吧!”

The Master said,“It is only Hui who could never be flagging when I spoke anything to him.”

[原文] **9·21 子谓颜渊,曰:“惜乎!吾见其进也,未见其止也。”**

[译文] 孔子谈到颜渊,说道:“他死了可惜呀!我只看见他进步,从没看见他停滞不前。”

The Master said of Yan Yuan,“What a pity that he has died! I have seen him go on, but never have I seen him stop.”

[原文] **9·22** 子曰:“苗而不秀者有矣夫!秀而不实者有矣夫!”

[译文] 孔子说:“庄稼不吐穗开花的有过的吧!吐穗开花却不结实的有过的吧!”

The Master said,“There are sprouts which can spring up but never flower; there are others which can flower but never bear fruit.”

[原文] **9·23** 子曰:“后生可畏,焉知来者之不如今也?四十、五十而无闻焉,斯亦不足畏也已。”

[译文] 孔子说:“年轻人是可敬畏的,怎能断定他们将来赶不上现在的人呢?四、五十岁还没有什么名望,也就不值得敬畏了。”

The Master said,“Awe is due to the youth. How do we know that their future will not be equal to our present? To men of forty or fifty, who have not made themselves heard of yet, no awe is due.”

[原文] **9·24** 子曰:“法语之言,能无从乎?改之为贵。巽与之言,能无说乎?绎之为贵。说而不绎,从而不改,吾末如之何也已矣。”

[译文] 孔子说:“合于礼法的正言规劝,能够不接受吗?改正错误才可贵。顺从自己的话,能够不高兴吗?分析研究一下才可贵。只高兴,不加分析研究,表面接受,实际不改,这种人我是没有办法对付他的了。”

The Master said,“Who would not give ear to the strict words

conforming to the rules of propriety? But to reform his conduct is praisable. Who would not be pleased by flattering words? But to ponder these words is praisable. With those who give ear but will not reform his conduct, who are pleased but will not ponder, I can really do nothing."

[原文] **9·25 子曰:"主忠信,毋友不如己者,过则勿惮改。"**

[译文] 孔子说:"应以忠心和信实两种品德为主,不要跟不如自己的人交朋友,有了过错就不要怕改正。"

The Master said, "Hold faithfulness and sincerity as first principles. Do not make friends with those who are not as good as you. When you have faults, you must not fear to correct them."

[原文] **9·26 子曰:"三军可夺帅也,匹夫不可夺志也。"**

[译文] 孔子说:"一个国家的军队,可以夺去它的主帅,一个普通的人,却不可能强迫他改变志向。"

The Master said, "The commander of the army may be carried off, but the will of even a common man cannot be taken from him."

[原文] **9·27 子曰:"衣敝缊袍,与衣狐貉者立,而不耻者,其由也与?'不忮不求,何用不臧?'"子路终身诵之。子曰:"是道也,何足以臧?"**

[译文] 孔子说:"穿着破烂的丝棉袍和穿着狐貉裘的人一道站着,而不觉得惭愧的,恐怕只有仲由吧?《诗经》说:'不嫉妒,

不贪求,为什么不会好?'"子路听了,终生念着这两句诗。孔子说:"仅仅这个样子,怎样能够好得起来?"

The Master said, "Dressed in a tattered, quilted robe, standingby the side of men in furs, and yet not ashamed, it is only Zhong You who can do so. As it says in the Book of Poetry, 'Void of hatred and greed, what else but good does he do?'" Afterwards Zilu kept on repeating these lines, the Master said, "Those things are by no means sufficient to constitute perfect excellence."

[原文] **9·28 子曰:"岁寒,然后知松柏之后凋也。"**

[译文] 孔子说:"季节寒冷了,才知道松柏树是最后凋谢的。"

The Master said,"Only when the year becomes cold, do we know that the pine and cypress are the last to fade."

[原文] **9·29 子曰:"知者不惑,仁者不忧,勇者不惧。"**

[译文] 孔子说:"聪明的人不致疑惑,仁德的人没有忧愁,勇敢的人无所畏惧。"

The Master said,"The wise are free from doubts; the virtuous from anxiety; and the brave from fear."

[原文] **9·30 子曰:"可与共学,未可与适道;可与适道,未可与立;可与立,未可与权。"**

[译文] 孔子说:"可以在一起学习,但未必能一起走向道;可以一起走向道的,未必能一起坚持道而不变;可以一起坚持不变的,未必能一起权衡轻重、灵活处事。"

The Master said,"With some we can join in learning, but

not in the Way; with others we can join in the Way, but not in adhering to the Way; and with others again we can join in adhering to the Way, but not in weighing occurring events along with us."

[原文] **9·31** "唐棣之华,偏其反而。岂不尔思?室是远而。"子曰:"未之思也,夫何远之有?"

[译文] "唐棣的花朵,翩翩摇摆。难道我不想念你?只因为家住得太遥远。"孔子道:"你是不去想念,有什么遥远呢?"

As a poem reads, "How the flowers of the aspenplum flutter and turn! Do I not think of you? But your house is far away." The Master said, "Your thoughts were not really with him, or how could he be far away?"

乡党篇第十

[原文] **10·1** 孔子于乡党,恂恂如也,似不能言者。其在宗庙朝廷,便便言,唯谨尔。

[译文] 孔子在家乡,非常恭顺,好像不能说话的人。他在宗庙里或朝廷上,便明白而流畅地说话,只是很谨慎罢了。

Confucius, in his village, looked gentle and sincere, as if he were not able to speak. In the ancestorial temple or at court, he spoke readily but cautiously.

[原文] **10·2** 朝,与下大夫言,侃侃如也;与上大夫言,訚訚如也。君在,踧踖如也,与与如也。

[译文] 上朝廷,同下大夫说话,温和而快乐的样子;同上大夫说话,正直而恭敬的样子。君主临朝,恭敬而心中不安的样子,行步安详的样子。

At court when speaking with the officers of low rank, he looked affable and pleasant; when speaking with the officers of high rank, he looked upright and respectful. When the prince was present, his manner displayed respectful uneasiness; it was grave, but self-possessed.

[原文] **10·3** 君召使摈,色勃如也,足躩如也。揖所与立,左右手,衣前后,襜如也。趋进,翼如也。宾退,必复命曰:"宾不顾矣。"

[译文] 国君召孔子去接待外国的贵宾,他面色矜持庄重,脚步也

快起来。向两旁的人作揖,或者向左拱手,或者向右拱手,衣裳一俯一仰,都很整齐。快步向前,好像鸟儿舒展了翅膀。贵宾辞别以后,一定向国君报告说:"客人已经不回头了。"

When the prince summoned him to receive guests, his countenance was solemn, his steps were swift. He bowed left and right to those beside him, straightened his robes in front and behind, and hastened forward, with his arms spreading like wings of a bird. When the guest had left, he would report to the prince, "The guest is no longer looking back."

[原文]

10·4 入公门,鞠躬如也,如不容。

立不中门,行不履阈。

过位,色勃如也,足躩如也,其言似不足者。

摄齐升堂,鞠躬如也,屏气似不息者。

出,降一等,逞颜色,怡怡如也。

没阶,趋进,翼如也。

复其位,踧踖如也。

[译文]

孔子走进朝廷的门,谨慎而恭敬的样子,好像没有容身之地。

不站在门的中间,行走不踩门坎。

经过国君的空座位,面色便矜持庄重,脚步也快起来,说话好像中气不足似的。

提起下摆上堂,弯腰显出恭敬谨慎的样子,憋着气,好像是不呼吸似的。

走出来,下一级台阶,面色便放松起来,怡然自得的样子。

走完了阶级,快步向前,好像鸟儿舒展了翅膀。

回到自己的席位,显出恭敬而不安的样子。

Entering the palace gate he looked cautious and respectful,

as if there were no room for him.

He did not stand in the middle of the gate, nor tread on the threshold.

Passing the throne, his countenance was solemn, his steps became swift, and his words came out as if he hardly had breath to utter them.

Ascending the dais, he held up his robe, bowed his back and held in his breath, as if he dared not breathe.

Coming down, after descending the first step, his countenance relaxed and bore a pleased look.

From the foot of the steps he advanced rapidly, with his arms spreading like wings of a bird.

When again in his seat his manner still showed respectful uneasiness.

[原文] **10·5** 执圭,鞠躬如也,如不胜。上如揖,下如授。勃如战色,足蹜蹜如有循。

享礼,有容色。

私觌,愉愉如也。

[译文] 孔子出使外国,会见国君,拿着圭,恭敬谨慎的样子,好像举不起来,向上举,好像在作揖;向下拿,好像在交给别人。面色战战兢兢,脚步也紧凑细小,好像沿着一条狭窄的路走过。

举行献礼物的礼仪时,满脸和气。

以私人身分会见外国君主,显得很愉快。

When on an official mission to another state, the Master carried Gui①. He was respectful and cautious as if he were not able to lift it. He raised it as if he were making a bow. He lowered it as though he were making a presentation. He wore an awed look and dragged his feet, as though he were walking along a line.

When presenting ritual-gifts, he wore a placid appearance.

At the private audience, he looked cheerful.

[注释] ① Symbol of the ruler's feudal investiture.

[原文] **10·6** 君子不以绀緅饰,红紫不以为亵服。

当暑,袗絺绤,必表而出之。

缁衣,羔裘;素衣,麑裘;黄衣,狐裘。

亵裘长,短右袂。

必有寝衣,长一身有半。

狐貉之厚以居。

去丧,无所不佩。

非帷裳,必杀之。

羔裘玄冠不以吊。

吉月,必朝服而朝。

[译文] 君子不用天青色和铁灰色的料子作镶边,浅红色和紫色的料子不用来做平常在家穿的衣服。

在暑天,穿着粗的或者细的葛布单衣,但一定套在外面。

黑色的外衣配紫羔,白色的外衣配麑裘,黄色的外衣配狐裘。

平时在家的皮袄较长,右边的袖子短一些。

睡觉一定有小被,有一个半人身长。

用狐、貉皮的厚毛做坐垫。

服丧满了以后,什么东西都可以佩戴。

不是朝服和祭服,一定要剪裁。

紫羔和黑色礼帽,都不穿戴着去吊丧。

大年初一,一定穿着上朝的礼服去朝贺。

The superior man did not use purple or mauve in facings of his dress, nor did he use red or violet in his undress.

In hot weather he wore unlined linen clothes, but always over other garments.

Over lam-bskin he wore black; over fawn's fur he wore white, over fox-skin he wore yellow.

At home he wore a long fur robe, with the right sleeve short.

When sleeping he always had his quilt, which was half as long as his body.

The thick furs of the fox or badger were for cushions.

When out of mourning, he wore all his girdle-ornaments.

Except for court or sacrificial dress, his clothes must be cut.

He did not wear lamb's fur or a black cap on a visit of condolence.

On the first day of the year, he always went to court in full court dress.

[原文] **10·7** 齐,必有明衣,布。

齐必变食,居必迁坐。

[译文] 斋戒沐浴的时候,一定要有浴衣,用麻布做的。

斋戒的时候,一定改变平常的饮食,居住也一定搬移地方。

On fast days he always wore a bathrobe made of linen cloth, changed his food and moved from the place where he commonly slept.

[原文] **10·8** 食不厌精,脍不厌细。

食饐而餲,鱼馁而肉败,不食。色恶,不食。臭恶,不食。失饪,不食。不时,不食。割不正,不食。不得其酱,不食。

肉虽多,不使胜食气。

唯酒无量,不及乱。

沽酒市脯不食。

不撤姜食,不多食。

[译文] 粮食不嫌舂得精,鱼和肉不嫌切得细。

饭食霉烂发臭,鱼和肉腐烂,都不吃。食物颜色难看,不吃。气味难闻,不吃。烹调不当,不吃。不到该吃时候,不吃。不是按一定方法宰割的肉,不吃。没有调味的酱醋,不吃。

席上肉虽然很多,吃肉不超过主食。

只有酒不限量,却不至于喝醉。

买来的酒和肉干不吃。

吃完了,姜不撤除,但吃得不多。

He did not dislike to have his rice finely cleaned, nor to have his meat finely minced.

He did not eat sour or mouldy rice, putrid fish, or tainted meat. Anything discoloured, or of a bad smell or badly cooked, he would not eat. He did not eat when it was not the right time for meals. He did not eat meat which was not properly cut, nor a dish without its proper sauce.

Though there was lots of meat, he would not eat more meat than rice.

To wine alone he set no limit, but he did not drink till he was inebriated.

He did not drink bought wine, or eat ready-dried market-meat.

After the meal, ginger was not taken away, But he did not eat much.

[原文] **10·9** 祭于公,不宿肉。祭肉不出三日。出三日,不食之矣。

[译文] 参与国家的祭祀典礼,不把分到的祭肉留到第二天。别的祭肉留存不超过三天。若是存放过了三天,便不吃它了。

After sacrifice at the palace, he would not keep the meat which he received over night. The meat of other sacrifice he did not keep over three days. If kept longer it was not eaten.

[原文] **10·10** 食不语,寝不言。

[译文] 吃饭的时候不交谈,睡觉的时候不说话。

He did not talk at meals, nor speak when in bed.

[原文] **10·11** 虽蔬食菜羹,必祭,必齐如也。

[译文] 即使吃的是粗米饭、菜汤,临吃前也要先祭一祭,而且表情严肃恭敬。

Although his food was coarse rice and vegetable soup, he still would offer a little of it in sacrifice with a grave respectful air.

[原文] **10·12** 席不正,不坐。

[译文] 坐席不端正,不坐。

If his mat was not straight he did not sit on it.

[原文] **10·13** 乡人饮酒,杖者出,斯出矣。

[译文] 同本乡人喝酒,等老年人都散去了,自己才出去。

When drinking with the villagers, he left the feast only after the elders had gone out.

[原文] 10·14 乡人傩,朝服而立于阼阶。

[译文] 本地方的人迎神驱鬼,便穿着朝服站在东边的台阶上。

At the village exorcisms he put on his court dress and stood on the eastern steps.

[原文] 10·15 问人于他邦,再拜而送之。

[译文] 托人向外国的朋友问好送礼,便向受托者拜两次后送行。

When sending inquires to his friends in another state, he bowed twice and saw his messenger off.

[原文] 10·16 康子馈药,拜而受之。曰:“丘未达,不敢尝。”

[译文] 季康子给孔子送药,孔子作揖行礼后接受了。说:“我对药性不了解,不敢试服。”

When Ji Kang Zi sent him some medicine, he bowed and received it, saying,“I do not know it, I dare not taste it.”

[原文] 10·17 厩焚。子退朝,曰:“伤人乎?”不问马。

[译文] 马棚失火。孔子从朝廷回来,说:“伤了人吗?”没问到马。

His stables having been burnt, Confucius, on his return from the court, said,“Is anyone hurt? He did not ask about horses.”

[原文] 10·18 君赐食,必正席先尝之。君赐腥,必熟而

荐之。君赐生,必畜之。

侍食于君,君祭,先饭。

[译文] 国君赐给食品,一定摆正坐位先尝一尝。国君赐给生肉,一定煮熟了,先供奉祖先。国君赐给活物,一定畜养着。

侍奉国君吃饭,当国君举行饭前祭礼的时候,自己先吃饭。

When the prince sent him a present of food, he must set his mat straight, and taste it first. When the prince sent him raw meat, he must cook it and make a sacrificial offering. When the prince sent him a living beast, he must rear it.

When dining in attendance on the prince, the prince made the sacrificial offering, he ate first.

[原文] **10·19** 疾,君视之,东首,加朝服,拖绅。

[译文] 孔子病了,国君来探问,他头朝东,把上朝的礼服盖在身上,拖着大带。

When he was sick and the prince came to see him, he had his head to the east and had his court dress spread across him, with the girdle over it.

[原文] **10·20** 君命召,不俟驾行矣。

[译文] 国君召唤,孔子便不等待车辆驾好马,立即动身。

When summoned by the prince, he went at once without waiting for his carriage to be yoked.

[原文] **10·21** 入太庙,每事问。

[译文] 孔子到了周公庙,每件事都要询问。

When he entered the Grand Temple, he asked about everything.

[原文] **10·22** 朋友死,无所归,曰:"于我殡。"

[译文] 朋友死了,没有料理的人,孔子说:"丧葬由我来料理。"

When a friend died and nobody was in charge of his funeral, the Master said, "Leave the funeral to me."

[原文] **10·23** 朋友之馈,虽车马,非祭肉,不拜。

[译文] 朋友的馈赠,即使是车马,只要不是祭肉,不行礼。

When a friend sent him a gift, though it might be a carriage and horses, so long as it was not sacrificial meat, he would not bow.

[原文] **10·24** 寝不尸,居不客。

[译文] 孔子睡觉不像死尸一样仰天直躺,平日坐着,也不像接见客人或者自己做客人一样,两膝跪在席上。

When sleeping he did not lie like a corpse. At home he did not kneel on the mat as if receiving guests.

[原文] **10·25** 见齐衰者,虽狎,必变。见冕者与瞽者,虽亵,必以貌。

凶服者式之。式负版者。

有盛馔,必变色而作。

迅雷风烈必变。

[译文] 孔子看见穿齐衰孝服的人,即使极亲密的,也一定变得严肃。看见戴着礼帽和瞎了眼睛的人,即使很熟悉,也一定有礼貌。

遇着拿了送死人衣物的人，便在车中把身体微微地向前一俯，手伏着车前的横木致礼。遇见背负国家图籍的人，也手伏车前横木示礼。

有丰富的菜肴，一定改变神色，站立起来。

遇见迅雷、大风，一定改变神色。

On seeing anyone in mourning, though he might be a friend, the Master would put on a solemn expression; on seeing anyone in full dress, or a blind man, though he knew him well, he would show a polite attitude to him.

When seeing a man in mourning from his carriage, he would bow forward to the cross-bar; he also bowed over the crossbar to the census-bearers.

Before a particularly choice dainty he would change countenance and rise up.

On a sudden clap of thunder, or a violent gust of wind, he would change countenance.

[原文] **10·26** 升车，必正立，执绥。

车中，不内顾，不疾言，不亲指。

[译文] 孔子上车，一定先端正地站着，抓着扶手带登车。

在车中，不向内回顾，不很快地说话，不用手指指画画。

When mounting his carriage, he would stand straight and hold the cord.

When in the carriage, he did not look around, or speak hastily, or point with his hands.

[原文] **10·27** 色斯举矣，翔而后集。曰："山梁雌雉，

时哉时哉!”子路共之,三嗅而作。

[译文] 野鸡见到颜色不善就飞了,盘旋飞翔了一阵又聚集停在一处。孔子说:“山梁上的这些雌雉,得其时呀! 得其时呀!”子路向它们拱了拱手,野鸡又拍拍翅膀飞走了。

Seeing the countenance, the hen pheasants instantly rose, flew around and by and by settled. The Master said, “These hen pheasants on the hill-bridge! At their season! At their season!” Zilu made a motion to them. They spread their wings and flew away.

先进篇第十一

[原文] **11·1** 子曰:"先进于礼乐,野人也;后进于礼乐,君子也。如用之,则吾从先进。"

[译文] 孔子说:"先学习礼乐而后做官的,是普通读书人;先有了官位而后学习礼乐的,是卿大夫世家子弟。如果我选用人才,我主张选用先学习礼乐的。"

The Master said, "Those who learned ritual and music first and then took office were the common people; those who took office first and then learned ritual and music were the sons of officials. If I were to appoint someone, I favored the one who learned ritual and music first."

[原文] **11·2** 子曰:"从我于陈、蔡者,皆不及门也。"

[译文] 孔子说:"跟着我在陈国、蔡国之间忍饥受饿的人,都不在我这里了。"

The Master said, "None of those who were with me in the states of Chen and Cai come any more to my door!"

[原文] **11·3** 德行:颜渊,闵子骞,冉伯牛,仲弓。言语:宰我,子贡。政事:冉有,季路。文学:子游,子夏。

[译文] 孔子的学生德行好的:颜渊,闵子骞,冉伯牛,仲弓。能言善辩的:宰我,子贡。善于办理政事的:冉有,季路。熟悉古代文献的:子游,子夏。

Distinguished for their virtue, there were Yan Yuan, Min

Ziqian, Ran Boniu and Zhong Gong; for their ability in speech, Zai Wo and Zigong; for their administrative talents, Ran You and Ji Lu; for their literary acquirements, Ziyou and Zixia.

[原文]　**11·4　子曰:"回也非助我者也,于吾言无所不说。"**

[译文]　孔子说:"颜回不是对我有所帮助的人,他对我的话没有不喜欢的。"

The Master said, "I get no help from Hui. No words I say but delights him!"

[原文]　**11·5　子曰:"孝哉闵子骞!人不间于其父母昆弟之言。"**

[译文]　孔子说:"闵子骞真是孝顺呀!别人对于他父母兄弟称赞他的话,从无异议。"

The Master said, "Filial indeed is Min Ziqian! Other people can say nothing of him different from the praises by his parents and brothers."

[原文]　**11·6　南容三复白圭,孔子以其兄之子妻之。**

[译文]　南容把《诗经》中"白圭之玷,尚可磨也;斯言之玷,不可为也"这几句诗读了又读,孔子把他哥哥的女儿嫁给他。

Nan Rong was frequently repeating the lines in the Book of Poetry: "A flaw in a white sceptre-stone may be ground away, but for a flaw in speech, nothing can be done." Confucius married Nan Rong his elder brother's daughter.

[原文]　**11·7　季康子问:"弟子孰为好学?"孔子对曰:**

“有颜回者好学，不幸短命死矣，今也则亡。”

[译文] 季康子问道：“你学生中谁爱好学习？”孔子回答说：“有一个叫颜回的爱好学习，不幸短命死了，现在就没有了。”

Ji Kangzi asked which of his disciples loved learning. Confucius answered, “There was Hui. He loved learning. Unfortunately he was short-lived and died. Now there is no one.”

[原文] **11·8** 颜渊死，颜路请子之车以为之椁。子曰：“才不才，亦各言其子也。鲤也死，有棺而无椁。吾不徒行以为之椁。以吾从大夫之后，不可徒行也。”

[译文] 颜渊死了，他的父亲颜路请求孔子卖掉车子来替颜渊做外椁。孔子说：“不管有才能还是没有才能，也是各人自己的儿子。我的儿子鲤死了，只有内棺，没有外椁。我不能卖掉车子步行来替他做外椁。因为我还跟随在大夫之后，是不可以步行的。”

When Yan Yuan died, his lather Yan Lu asked for the Master's carriage to make an enclosure for his son's coffin. The Master said, “Whether gifted or not, each one speaks of his son. When my son Li died, he only had a coffin but no enclosure. I would not walk on foot to furnish an enclosure. Because, following after the great officers, it was not proper for me to walk on foot.”

[原文] **11·9** 颜渊死。子曰：“噫！天丧予！天丧予！”

[译文] 颜渊死了，孔子说：“唉！上天要我的命呀！上天要我的命呀！”

When Yan Yuan died, the Master said, “Alas! Heaven is destroying me! Heaven is destroying me!”

［原文］ **11·10 颜渊死，子哭之恸。从者曰："子恸矣！"曰："有恸乎？非夫人之为恸而谁为？"**

［译文］ 颜渊死了，孔子哭得非常悲痛，跟随孔子的人说："您太悲哀了！"孔子说："真的太悲哀了吗？我不为这样的人伤心，还为什么人伤心呢！"

When Yan Yuan died the Master gave way to grief. Those with him said, "Sir, your grief is excessive." The Master said, "Is it excessive? If for this man I did not give way to grief, for whom should I give way?"

［原文］ **11·11 颜渊死，门人欲厚葬之。子曰："不可。"**

门人厚葬之。子曰："回也视予犹父也，予不得视犹子也。非我也，夫二三子也。"

［译文］ 颜渊死了，孔子的学生们想要厚葬他。孔子说："不可以。"

学生们仍然厚葬了他。孔子说："颜回看待我好像父亲一样，我却不能够像对待儿子一样看待你。这不是我的主意呀，是你那帮同学干的呀。"

When Yan Yuan died the disciples wished to give him a great funeral, and the Master said, "You cannot do so."

The disciples did bury him in great style. The Master said, "Hui treated me as a father; I have failed to treat him as a son. No, it was not my idea. It was your doing, my disciples!"

［原文］ **11·12 季路问事鬼神。子曰："未能事人，焉能事鬼？"**

曰："敢问死。"曰："未知生，焉知死？"

［译文］ 子路问怎样事奉鬼神。孔子说："还没能服事活人，怎么能去服事鬼神呢？"

子路又说："我大胆地请问死是怎么回事。"孔子说："还没有弄明白生，怎么能够懂得死？"

Jilu asked about serving the spirits of the dead. The Master said, "While you are not able to serve the living, how can you serve their spirits?"

Jilu added, "I venture to ask about death." The Master said, "While you do not know life, how can you know about death?"

［原文］ **11·13** 闵子侍侧，訚訚如也；子路，行行如也；冉有、子贡，侃侃如也。子乐。"若由也，不得其死然。"

［译文］ 闵子骞站在孔子身旁，恭敬而正直的样子；子路很刚强的样子；冉有、子贡温和而快乐的样子。孔子高兴了。但又说："像仲由吧，怕得不到好死。"

Standing by the side of the Master, Min Ziqian looked respectful and honest; Zilu looked bold and soldierly; Ran You and Zigong looked genial and pleasant. The Master was pleased. But he said, "A man like Zhong You, will not die a natural death."

［原文］ **11·14** 鲁人为长府。闵子骞曰："仍旧贯，如之何？何必改作？"子曰："夫人不言，言必有中。"

［译文］ 鲁国翻修叫长府的金库。闵子骞说："依旧照着老样子，怎么样？为什么一定要翻修呢？"孔子说："这个人平日不说话，一开口一定说得正确。"

The Men of Lu were rebuilding the treasury of Changfu, Min

Ziqian said, "Would not the old one do? Why must a new one be built?" The Master said, "That man seldom speaks; when he does, he is sure to hit the point."

[原文] **11·15** 子曰:"由之瑟奚为于丘之门?"门人不敬子路。子曰:"由也升堂矣,未入于室也。"

[译文] 孔子说:"仲由弹瑟为什么到我这里来弹奏呢?"孔子的学生们因此不尊敬子路。孔子说:"仲由在学问上已经是升堂了,只是还没入室罢了。"

The Master said, "Why does Zhong You play Se① in my house?" Whereupon the other disciples began not to respect Zilu. The Master said, "In learning Zhong You has ascended to the hall, but he has not yet entered the inner rooms."

[注释] ① A large horizontal musical instrument.

[原文] **11·16** 子贡问:"师与商也孰贤?"子曰:"师也过,商也不及。"

曰:"然则师愈与?"子曰:"过犹不及。"

[译文] 子贡问孔子:"颛孙师和卜商,谁好一些?"孔子说:"颛孙师有些过分,卜商有些赶不上。"

子贡说:"那么,颛孙师好一些吗?"孔子说:"过分和赶不上同样不好。"

Zigong asked, "Who is the better, Shi ①or Shang②?" The Master said, "Shi goes too far; Shang goes not far enough."

Zigong said, "Then Shi is the better, I suppose." The Master said, "Too far is no better than not far enough."

[注释] ① i. e. Zizhang.

② i. e. Zixia.

[原文] **11·17** 季氏富于周公，而求也为之聚敛而附益之。子曰："非吾徒也。小子鸣鼓而攻之，可也。"

[译文] 季氏比周公还富足，冉求又替他搜括，增加更多的财富。孔子说："冉求不是我的学生，你们学生可以大张旗鼓地攻击他。"

The head of the Ji family was richer than the Duke of Zhou, and yet Ran Qiu collected taxes for him and increased his wealth. The Master said, "He is no disciple of mine. My disciples, beat the drum and assail him."

[原文] **11·18** 柴也愚，参也鲁，师也辟，由也喭。

[译文] 高柴愚笨，曾参迟钝，颛孙师偏激，仲由卤莽。

Chai[①] is stupid, Shen is dull, Shi is extreme, Zhong You is rash.

[注释] ① Gao Chai, disciple of Confucius.

[原文] **11·19** 子曰："回也其庶乎，屡空。赐不受命，而货殖焉，億则屡中。"

[译文] 孔子说："颜回的学问道德差不多了吧，可是常常穷得什么也没有。端木赐不听天由命，去囤积投机，猜测行情，竟每每猜对了。"

The Master said, "Hui has nearly attained perfect virtue, but he is often in want. Ci does not bow to fate. He engages in speculation and cornering. In his calculations he often hits the mark."

[原文] **11·20** 子张问善人之道。子曰："不践迹，亦不入

于室。”

[译文] 子张问怎样做个善人。孔子说:“善人不踩着别人的脚印走,但是,学问道德也难以长进到家。”

Zizhang asked what was the way of a good man. The Master said, “He does not tread in the footsteps of others, nor do his virtue and learning attain to perfection.”

[原文] **11·21** 子曰:“论笃是与,君子者乎? 色庄者乎?”

[译文] 孔子说:“人们总是赞扬说话诚实的人,但这种人是真正的君子呢? 还是神情外表庄重的人呢?”

The Master said, “People always approve of a man whose discourse seems solid and sincere. But is he really a superior man, or one who merely adopts outward airs of solemnity?”

[原文] **11·22** 子路问:“闻斯行诸?”子曰:“有父兄在,如之何其闻斯行之?”

冉有问:“闻斯行诸?”子曰:“闻斯行之。”

公西华曰:“由也问闻斯行诸,子曰‘有父兄在’;求也问闻斯行诸,子曰‘闻斯行之’。赤也惑,敢问。”子曰:“求也退,故进之;由也兼人,故退之。”

[译文] 子路问:“听到就干起来吗?”孔子说:“有父亲和兄长活着,怎么能听到就干起来?”

冉有问:“听到就干起来吗?”孔子说:“听到就干起来。”

公西华说:“仲由问听到就干起来吗,您说‘有父亲和兄长活着’;冉求问听到就干起来吗,您说‘听到就干起来’。我有些糊涂,大胆地请问这是为什么?”孔子说:“冉求平日做事退缩,所以我向前推动他;仲由的胆量有两个人的大,所以我要让他向后退缩。”

Zilu asked, “Shall I immediately put into practice what I heard? The Master said, “While your father and elder brother are alive, how can you immediately put what you heard into practice?”

Ran You asked, “Shall I immediately put into practice what I heard?” The Master said, “Immediately put into practice what you heard.”

Gongxi Hua said, “Zhong You asked whether he should do immediately what he heard and you said, ‘While your father and elder brothers are alive.’ Qiu asked whether he should do immediately what he heard, and you said, ‘Immediately put into practice what you heard.’ I am confused, and venture to ask you.” The Master said, “Qiu is bashful, so I egged him on; Zhong You has the plack of two, so I held him back.”

［原文］ **11·23** 子畏于匡，颜渊后。子曰：“吾以女为死矣。”曰：“子在，回何敢死？”

［译文］ 孔子在匡地被囚禁，颜渊最后才来。孔子说：“我以为你死了。”颜渊说：“您还活着，我怎么敢死呢？”

The Master was trapped in Kuang and Yan Hui fell behind. The Master said, “I thought you had died.” Hui replied, “While you are alive, how shall I dare to die?”

［原文］ **11·24** 季子然问：“仲由、冉求可谓大臣与？”子曰：“吾以子为异之问，曾由与求之问。所谓大臣者，以道事君，不可则止。今由与求也，可谓具臣矣。”

曰:“然则从之者与?”子曰:“弑父与君,亦不从也。”

[译文] 季子然问:“仲由和冉求可以说是大臣吗?”孔子说:“我以为你是问别的人,竟只是问仲由和冉求。我们所说的大臣,是用正确的原则来事奉君主,行不通,就不干。如今仲由和冉求,可以说是具有相当才能的臣属了。”

季子然又说:“那么,他们会一切都顺从上级吗?”孔子说:“杀父亲、杀君主的事情,他们是不会顺从的。”

Ji Ziran asked whether Zhong You and Ran Qiu could be called great ministers. The Master said,“I thought you would ask about somebody else, and you ask only about Zhong You and Qiu! What is called a great minister, is one who serves his prince according to what is right, and when he finds he cannot do so, retires. Now, as for Zhong You and Qiu, they may be called ordinary ministers.”

Ji Ziran said,“Then they will always follow their chief, will they”The Master said,“In an act of slaying their prince or their father, they would not follow him.”

[原文] 11·25 子路使子羔为费宰。子曰:“贼夫人之子。”

子路曰:“有民人焉,有社稷焉,何必读书,然后为学?”

子曰:“是故恶夫佞者。”

[译文] 子路派子羔去做费县县长。孔子说:“这是害了这个年轻人了。”

子路说:“那地方有老百姓,有土地和五谷,为什么一定要读书才叫做学习呢?”

孔子说："所以我讨厌尖嘴利舌的人。"

Zilu made Zigao① governor of Fei. The Master said, "You are doing harm to this young man."

Zilu said, "There are the people, there are the altars of the spirits of the land and grain there: why only reading can be called learning?" The Master said, "This is why I hate glibtongued people."

[注释] ① i. e. Gao Chai.

[原文] **11·26** 子路、曾皙、冉有、公西华侍坐。

子曰："以吾一日长乎尔，毋吾以也。居则曰：'不吾知也！'如或知尔，则何以哉？"

子路率尔而对曰："千乘之国，摄乎大国之间，加之以师旅，因之以饥馑，由也为之，比及三年，可使有勇，且知方也。"

夫子哂之。

"求，尔何如？"

对曰："方六七十，如五六十，求也为之，比及三年，可使足民。如其礼乐，以俟君子。"

"赤，尔何如？"

对曰："非曰能之，愿学焉。宗庙之事，如会同，端章甫，愿为小相焉。"

"点，尔何如？"

鼓瑟希，铿尔，舍瑟而作，对曰："异乎三子者之撰。"

子曰："何伤乎？亦各言其志也。"

曰："莫春者，春服既成，冠者五六人，童子六七人，浴乎沂，风乎舞雩，咏而归。”

夫子喟然叹曰：“吾与点也！”

三子者出，曾皙后。曾皙曰：“夫三子者之言何如？”

子曰：“亦各言其志也已矣。”

曰：“夫子何哂由也？”

曰：“为国以礼，其言不让，是故哂之。”

“唯求则非邦也与？”

“安见方六七十如五六十而非邦也者？”

“唯赤则非邦也与？”

“宗庙会同，非诸侯而何？赤也为之小，孰能为之大？”

［译文］ 子路、曾皙、冉有、公西华四个人陪着孔子坐着。

孔子说：“因为我比你们年纪都大一些，（老了，）不要因为我年长而不敢说。你们平常说：‘人家不知道我呀！’假如有人了解你们，那你们怎么办呢？”

子路急忙轻率地回答：“一千辆兵车的国家，在大国之间受逼迫，外面有军队侵犯它，加上国内又闹灾荒。我如果去治理，三年以后，可使人人有勇气，而且懂得礼义。”

孔子微微一笑。

又问：“冉求，你怎么样？”

冉求回答说：“国土纵横各六七十里或者五六十里的小国家，我去治理，等到三年，可使人民富足。至于礼乐教化，那只有等待贤人君子了。”

又问：“公西赤，你怎么样？”

公西赤回答说：“不是说我有本领，但我愿意学习。在宗庙举行祭祀，或者同外国盟会，我愿意穿着礼服，戴着礼帽，做一个小司仪。”

又问：“曾点，你怎么样？”

他弹瑟接近尾声，铿的一声把瑟放下，站了起来，回答说：“我的志向和他们三位所讲的不同。”

孔子说：“那有什么关系呢？只是各人说说自己的志向罢了！”

曾皙便说：“暮春三月，春天衣服都穿上了，我陪同五六位成年人，六七个小孩，在沂水旁边洗洗澡，在舞雩台上吹吹风，一路唱着歌走回来。”

孔子长叹一声说：“我同意曾点的想法啊！”

子路、冉有、公西华三人都退了出去，曾皙走在后面。曾皙说：“那三位的话怎么样？”

孔子说：“也不过各人说说自己的志向罢了。”

曾皙又说：“您为什么笑仲由呢？”

孔子说：“治理国家应该讲求礼让，可是他的话却一点不谦虚，所以笑他。”

“难道冉求所讲的就不是国家吗？”

孔子说：“怎见得纵横各六七十里或者五六十里的土地就不是一个国家呢？”

“公西赤所讲的不是国家吗？”

孔子说：“有宗庙，有国际的盟会，不是国家是什么？公西赤如果他只能做一个小司仪，谁能够做大司仪呢？”

Zilu, Zeng Xi①, Ran You, and Gongxi Hua were sitting by the Master.

The Master said, “I may be older than you, but do not think of that. You often say, ‘We are not known.’ Well, if some prince were to know you, what would you do?”

Zilu hastily and lightly answered, “Give me charge of a state of a thousand chariots, hemmed in by powerful neighbours, invaded by foreign armies, and searched by famine at home, in three years'time I could make the people bold, and recognize the rules of righteous conduct."

The Master smiled.

"What would you do, Qiu?" he asked.

Qiu answered, "Had I charge a state of sixty or seventy square miles, or one of fifty or sixty, in three years'time I could give the people plenty. As to teaching ritual and music, I would wait for the rise of a superior man to do that."

"And what would you do, Chi?"

Chi answered. "I speak of the things I would like to learn, not of what I can do. At service in the ancestral temple, or at the audience of the princes, I would like, in full dress, to act as a small assistant."

"And what would you do, Dian②?"

Dian ceased to play, pushed his still sounding Se aside, rose and answered, "My wishes are different from those of the other three."

The Master said, "What harm in that? Each but speak his mind."

Zeng Xi said, "In the last days of spring, with the dress of the season all complete, along with five or six young men and six or seven boys, I would bathe in the Yi River, enjoy the breeze at Wuyu (the Rain Dance altar), and return home singing."

The Master sighed and said, "I am with Dian."

The three others having gone out, Zeng Xi remained behind, and said, "What do you think of what the others said?"

"Each but speak his mind," said the Master.

"Why did you smile at Zhong You?"

"The management of a state demands the rules of propriety, but what he said was not modest. That was why I smiled at him."

"But did not Qiu speak of a state?"

"Did you ever see a territory of sixty or seventy square miles, or one of fifty or sixty, which was not a state?"

"And did not Chi, too, speak of a state?"

"Who but princes would there be in the Ancestral Temple, or at the Grand Audience? If Chi were to be a small assistant in these services, who could be a great one?"

[注释]

① The father of Zeng Zi, disciple of Confucius.

② i. e. Zeng Xi.

颜渊篇第十二

［原文］ **12·1** 颜渊问仁。子曰:“克己复礼为仁。一日克己复礼,天下归仁焉。为仁由己,而由人乎哉?”

颜渊曰:“请问其目。”子曰:“非礼勿视,非礼勿听,非礼勿言,非礼勿动。”

颜渊曰:“回虽不敏,请事斯语矣。”

［译文］ 颜渊问什么是仁。孔子说:“克制自己,使言语行动都合于礼,就是仁。一旦这样做到了,天下的人都会称许你是仁人。实践仁德,全靠自己,还靠别人吗?”

颜渊说:“请问实行仁德的具体条目。”孔子说:“不合礼的不看,不合礼的不听,不合礼的不说,不合礼的不做。”

颜渊说:“我虽然迟钝,也要按照您这些话去实行。”

Yan Yuan asked about perfect virtue. The Master said, “To subdue one’s-self and turn to propriety is perfect virtue. If a man can subdue himself and turn to propriety, everyone under heaven would praise him as a man of perfect virtue. The practice of perfect virtue is from a man himself, is it from others?”

Yan Yuan said, “May I ask for the more detailed items of this?” The Master said, “Do not look at what is contrary to propriety; do not listen to what is contrary to propriety; do not speak what is contrary to propriety ;do not do what is contrary to propriety.”

Yan Yuan then said, “Though I am dull, I hope to live by these words.”

[原文] **12·2** 仲弓问仁。子曰:“出门如见大宾,使民如承大祭。己所不欲,勿施于人。在邦无怨,在家无怨。”

仲弓曰:“雍虽不敏,请事斯语矣。”

[译文] 仲弓问什么是仁。孔子说:“出门工作好像去接待贵宾,役使百姓好像去承当大的祀典。自己不喜欢的,不强加给别人。在工作职位上无所怨恨,不在工作职位上也无所怨恨。”

仲弓说:“我虽然不聪敏,也要照您这话去做。”

Zhonggong asked about perfect virtue. The Master said, “When away from home, to behave as though you were receiving a great guest; to employ the people as though you were assisting at a great sacrifice; do not do to others what you do not wish yourself; do not bear resentment either in the state or in the family.”

Zhonggong said, “Though I am dull, I hope to live by these words.”

[原文] **12·3** 司马牛问仁。子曰:“仁者,其言也讱。”

曰:“其言也讱,斯谓之仁已乎?”子曰:“为之难,言之得无讱乎?”

[译文] 司马牛问什么是仁。孔子说:“仁人,他的言语迟钝。”

司马牛说:“言语迟钝,这就叫做仁了吗?”孔子说:“做起来很难,说起来能够不迟钝吗?”

Sima Niu asked about perfect virtue. The Master said, “The man of perfect virtue is cautious and slow in his speech.”

“Cautious and slow in his speech!” said Niu, “is this what is meant by perfect virtue?” The Master said, “That which is hard to do, can it be lightly spoken?”

[原文] **12·4 司马牛问君子。子曰:“君子不忧不惧。”曰:“不忧不惧,斯谓之君子已乎?”子曰:“内省不疚,夫何忧何惧?”**

[译文] 司马牛问怎样做一个君子。孔子说:“君子不忧愁,不恐惧。”

司马牛说:“不忧愁,不恐惧,这就叫做君子了吗?”孔子说:“内心反省自己毫不愧疚,有什么可忧愁、可害怕的呢?”

Sima Niu asked what is a superior man. The Master said, “A superior man has neither anxiety nor fear.”

“No anxiety and no fear!” said Niu, “Does this constitute what we call a superior man?” The Master said, “When internal examination finds nothing wrong, what should he be anxious about? What should he fear?”

[原文] **12·5 司马牛忧曰:“人皆有兄弟,我独亡。”子夏曰:“商闻之矣:死生有命,富贵在天。君子敬而无失,与人恭而有礼。四海之内,皆兄弟也。君子何患乎无兄弟也?”**

[译文] 司马牛忧愁地说:“别人都有兄弟,单单我没有。”子夏道:“我听说过:死生听之命运,富贵由天安排。君子只是对待工作严肃认真,不出差错,对待别人恭谨,合乎礼节,天下到处都是兄弟,君子又何必担忧没有兄弟呢?”

Sima Niu said sadly, “All men have brothers, I alone have none!” Zixia said, “I have heard that life and death are determined by fate, that wealth and honours depend upon the will of Heaven. A superior man attends to business carefully and does not trip; he is respectful to others and observant of propriety. All within the world will be his brothers. How can a superior man feel distressed about his lack of them?"

[原文] **12·6** 子张问明。子曰:"浸润之谮,肤受之愬,不行焉,可谓明也已矣。浸润之谮,肤受之愬,不行焉,可谓远也已矣。"

[译文] 子张问什么是明智。孔子说:"点滴而来、日积月累的谗言和肌肤所受、切身之痛的诬告,在你这里行不通,那你可以说是明智了。点滴而来、日积月累的谗言和肌肤所受、切身之痛的诬告,在你这里行不通,可以说是有远见的了。"

Zizhang asked what constituted intelligence. The Master said, "He who is influenced neither by slander that gradually soaks into the mind, nor by calumny that startles like a wound in the flesh, may be called intelligent indeed. Yes, he is influenced neither by soaking slander nor by startling calumny may be called far-sighted."

[原文] **12·7** 子贡问政。子曰:"足食,足兵,民信之矣。"

子贡曰:"必不得已而去,于斯三者何先?"曰:"去兵。"

子贡曰:"必不得已而去,于斯二者何先?"曰:"去食。自古皆有死,民无信不立。"

[译文] 子贡问怎样治理国家。孔子说:"粮食充足,军备充足,民众对政府便信赖了。"

子贡说:"如果迫不得已在粮食、军备、民众信赖三项之中要去掉一项,先去掉哪一项?"孔子说:"不要军备。"

子贡说:“如果迫不得已,在粮食和人民信赖两者之中要去掉一项,去掉哪一项呢?”孔子说:“不要粮食。自古以来,谁都免不了一死,失去人民的信赖,政府便站不住脚了。”

Zigong asked about government. The Master said, “Sufficient food, sufficient military equipment, and the confidence of the people in their ruler.”

Zigong said, “If it cannot be helped, and one of these three must be dispensed with, which should be forgone first?” “The military equipment,” said the Master.

Zigong asked, “If it cannot be helped, and one of the remaining two must be dispensed with, which should be forgone?” The Master said, “Food. From of old, death has been the lot of all men; but if the people have no confidence in their ruler, a state cannot stand.”

[原文] **12·8 棘子成曰:“君子质而已矣,何以文为?”子贡曰:“惜乎,夫子之说君子也!驷不及舌。文犹质也,质犹文也。虎豹之鞟犹犬羊之鞟。”**

[译文] 棘子成说:“君子只要本质好就行了,要什么文彩呢?”子贡说:“遗憾啊,先生这样谈论君子!一言既出,驷马难追。文彩如同本质,本质也如同文彩,二者是同样重要的。把虎豹和犬羊身上有文彩的毛都拔去,它们的皮革就一样了。”

Ji Zicheng said, “Only the substantial qualities are wanted in a superior man. What can ornamental accomplishments do for him?” The Master said, “I'm sorry, sir, that you spoke of a superior man in such a way. Even a team of four horses cannot overtake and recover what is already said. Ornament is as substance;

substance is as ornament. Without the fur, a tiger or a leopard's hide is like the hide of a dog, or goat."

[原文]

12·9 哀公问于有若曰:"年饥,用不足,如之何?"

有若对曰:"盍彻乎?"

曰:"二,吾犹不足,如之何其彻也?"

对曰:"百姓足,君孰与不足?百姓不足,君孰与足?"

[译文]

鲁哀公问有若说:"年成歉收,国家费用不够,怎么办?"

有若回答说:"何不实行十分抽一的税率呢?"

鲁哀公说:"十分抽二我都不够,怎么能十分抽一呢?"

有若回答说:"如果百姓费用够,您怎么会不够?如果百姓费用不够,您怎么会够?"

Duke Ai said to You Rou, "In this year of dearth, the state has not enough for needs; what should be done?"

You Rou answered, "Why not levy a one-tenth tax on people?"

"With two tenths," said the duke, "I find them not enough, how could the system of one tenth avail?"

You Rou said, "When the people all live in plenty, will the prince alone be in want? If the people are all in want, can the prince alone live in plenty?"

[原文]

12·10 子张问崇德辨惑。子曰:"主忠信,徙义,崇德也。爱之欲其生,恶之欲其死。既欲其生,又欲其死,是惑也。'诚不以富,亦只以异。'"

[译文]

子张问怎么样提高品德,释疑辨惑,孔子说:"以忠诚信实为主,凡事按情理去干,这就能提高品德。喜爱一个人,希望他长命百岁,厌恶一个人,便恨不得他立刻死去。既要他长寿,又要他死去,这便是迷惑。'这样,对自己毫无好处,只是使人家奇怪罢了。'"

Zizhang asked how to exalt virtue and scatter delusion. The Master said, "Hold faithfulness and sincerity as first principles, and follow righteousness; your virtue will be exalted. You love a man and wish him to live; you hate him, and wish him to die. To wish him both life and death is a case of delusion. 'It was no help to himself, but only made others confused.'"

[原文] **12·11** 齐景公问政于孔子。孔子对曰:"君君,臣臣,父父,子子。"公曰:"善哉!信如君不君,臣不臣,父不父,子不子,虽有粟,吾得而食诸?"

[译文] 齐景公问孔子怎样治理国家。孔子回答说:"国君要像个国君,臣子要像个臣子,父亲要像个父亲,儿子要像个儿子。"齐景公说:"好呀!假若国君真不像个国君,臣子真不像个臣子,父亲真不像个父亲,儿子真不像个儿子,即使有粮食,我能够吃得着吗?"

Duke Jing of Qi asked Confucius about government. Confucius said, "Let the ruler be ruler, the minister minister, the father father, and the son son." "True indeed!" said the duke, "If the ruler is not ruler, the minister not minister, the father not father, and the son not son, although the abundant grain was there, could I get enough to eat?"

[原文] **12·12** 子曰:"片言可以折狱者,其由也与?"

子路无宿诺。

［译文］ 孔子说:“根据单方面的话,就可以判决诉讼案件的,恐怕只有仲由吧?”

子路从不拖延履行诺言。

The Master said, “It is only Zhong You who could settle lawsuits on hearing one-sideded words!”

Zilu never slept over a promise.

［原文］ **12·13** 子曰:“听讼,吾犹人也。必也使无讼乎!”

［译文］ 孔子说:“审理诉讼,我和别人差不多。但一定要使诉讼案件没有才好。”

The Master said, “At hearing lawsuits I am like anybody else. What is necessary is to cause the people to have no lawsuits.”

［原文］ **12·14** 子张问政。子曰:“居之无倦,行之以忠。”

［译文］ 子张问怎样做官。孔子说:“在职位上不疲沓偷懒,办起公事忠实尽力。”

Zizhang asked about government. The Master said, “To be tireless and faithful in carrying on your government.”

［原文］ **12·15** 子曰:“博学于文,约之以礼,亦可以弗畔矣夫!”

［译文］ 孔子说:“君子广泛地学习文献,再用礼节来约束,也就可以不致于离经叛道了。”

The Master said, “He who is widely versed in letters and keeps himself under the restraint of propriety may thus not overstep what is right."

[原文] **12·16** 子曰:"君子成人之美,不成人之恶。小人反是。"

[译文] 孔子说:"君子成全别人的好事,不促成别人的坏事。小人和这相反。"

The Master said, "A superior man helps fulfil other's cherished hopes; he does not help fulfil other's cherished evils. The small man does the opposite of this."

[原文] **12·17** 季康子问政于孔子。孔子对曰:"政者,正也。子帅以正,孰敢不正?"

[译文] 季康子向孔子问什么是政治。孔子说:"政治的意思是端正。您带头端正行为,谁敢不端正呢?"

Ji Kang Zi asked Confucius about government, The Master said, "To rule is to set straight. If you give an upright lead, who will dare walk crooked?"

[原文] **12·18** 季康子患盗,问于孔子。孔子对曰:"苟子之不欲,虽赏之不窃。"

[译文] 季康子苦于盗贼太多,向孔子求教。孔子说:"如果您不贪图财货,就是奖赏他们,他们也不会去偷窃。"

Ji Kang Zi, being vexed by thieves, spoke of it to Confucius. Confucius said, "If you, sir, were not greedy, though you should reward thieves, no one would steal."

[原文] **12·19** 季康子问政于孔子曰:"如杀无道,以就有

道,何如?”孔子对曰:“子为政,焉用杀?子欲善而民善矣。君子之德风,小人之德草。草上之风,必偃。”

[译文] 季康子向孔子求教怎样治理国家,说:“假若杀掉坏人来亲近好人,怎么样?”孔子回答说:“您治理国家哪里一定用得着杀人?您想搞好,百姓自然会好。领导人的德行好比是风,老百姓的德行好比是草。风从草上吹过,草必定向一边倒。”

Ji Kang Zi asked Confucius about government, saying, “What do you think of killing the bad so as to help on the good?” Confucius answered, “Sir, in carrying on your government, why should you use killing at all? Were you set on good, sir, your people would do good. The superiors’virtue is the wind, the inferiors’virtue is grass. Wherever the wind blows, grass bends.”

[原文] **12·20** 子张问:“士何如斯可谓之达矣?”子曰:“何哉,尔所谓达者?”子张对曰:“在邦必闻,在家必闻。”子曰:“是闻也,非达也。夫达也者,质直而好义,察言而观色,虑以下人。在邦必达,在家必达。夫闻也者,色取仁而行违,居之不疑。在邦必闻,在家必闻。”

[译文] 子张问:“读书人怎样做才能叫通达?”孔子说:“你所说的通达是什么意思?”子张说:“在国家的职位上一定有名望,作大夫的家臣一定有名望。”孔子说:“这是名望,不是通达。怎样才能叫通达呢?品质正直,遇事做得合情理,善于分析别人的话语,观察别人的颜色,每每考虑到谦让,不居于别人之上。这种人,在国家的职位上一定事事行得通,在大夫家臣的职位上也一定事事行得通。至于所谓有名望,表面上似乎爱好仁德,实际行为背道而驰,自己却以仁人自居,而不加怀疑。

这种人,在国家的职位上一定会骗取名望,在大夫家臣的职位上也一定会骗取名望。"

Zi Zhang asked, "When may a scholar be called eminent?" The Master said, "What do you mean by eminence?" Zizhang answered, "It is to be heard of through the state, and to be heard of through the family." The Master said, "That is fame, not eminence. The eminent man is straightforward, and loves righteousness. He examines man's words and observes their expressions. He bears in mind the necessity of deferring to others. Such a man will be eminent in the state, and eminent in the family. A famous man wears a mask of righteousness, his conduct belies it. And he rests in this character without doubts about himself. Such a man will be heard of in the state, he will be heard of in the family."

[原文] **12·21 樊迟从游于舞雩之下,曰:"敢问崇德,修慝,辨惑。"子曰:"善哉问!先事后得,非崇德与?攻其恶,无攻人之恶,非修慝与?一朝之忿,忘其身,以及其亲,非惑与?"**

[译文] 樊迟陪侍孔子在舞雩台下游览,说:"我大胆地问,怎样去提高自己的品德,消除别人不曾表露出来的隐怨,辨别哪些是糊涂事?"孔子说:"问得好!工作在先,收获在后,这不足以提高自己的品德吗?抨击自己的坏处,不抨击别人的坏处,这不就可以消除隐怨吗?因为一时偶然的愤怒,便忘掉自己,甚至也忘掉父母,岂不是糊涂吗?"

While wandering through the Wuyu altar with the Master, Fan Chi said to him, "May I ask how to exalt virtue, to remove hidden resentment, and discover delusions?" The Master said, "A good question! Rate the task above the prize, will not the virtue be exalted? Assail one's own evil, not the evil of others, will not hidden resentment be removed? For a morning's anger, to disregard one's life, and involve that of parents, is not this a case of delusion?"

[原文] **12·22** 樊迟问仁。子曰:"爱人。"问知。子曰:"知人。"

樊迟未达。子曰:"举直错诸枉,能使枉者直。"

樊迟退,见子夏曰:"乡也吾见于夫子而问知,子曰'举直错诸枉,能使枉者直',何谓也?"

子夏曰:"富哉言乎!舜有天下,选于众,举皋陶,不仁者远矣。汤有天下,选于众,举伊尹,不仁者远矣。"

[译文] 樊迟问什么是仁。孔子说:"爱护别人。"他又问什么是智。孔子说:"善于鉴别人物。"

樊迟不很理解。孔子说:"提拔正直的人,官位在不正派的人之上,便能使不正派的人也正直。"

樊迟退了出来,看见子夏,说:"刚才我见到老师,问什么是智,他老人家说,'提拔正直的人,官位在不正派的人之上,能使不正派的人也正直。'这是什么意思?"

子夏说:"这话的意义多么丰富呀!舜得天下,在众人中挑选人才,任用皋陶,不仁的人就远离了。汤得天下,在众人中挑选人才,任用伊尹,不仁的人就远离了。"

Fan Chi asked about human-heartedness. The Master said, "To love all people." He asked about wisdom. The Master said, "To know all people."

Fan Chi did not understand. The Master said, "Promote the upright and put them above the crooked, the crooked can be made to be upright."

Fan Chi withdrew, meeting Zixia, said to him, "Just now I had an interview with our Master and asked him about wisdom. The Master said, 'Promote the upright, put them above the crooked; the crooked can be made to be upright.' What did he mean?"

Zixia said, "How rich is his saying! When Shun was in possession of the world, he chose Gao Yao from the many, exalted him, and men without virtue disappeared. When Tang was in possession of the world, he chose Yi Yin from the many, exalted him, and men without virtue disappeared."

[原文] **12·23** 子贡问友。子曰:"忠告而善道之,不可则止,毋自辱焉。"

[译文] 子贡问怎样对待朋友。孔子说:"诚心诚意地告诫他,好心地开导他,他不听就算了,不要自找侮辱。"

Zigong asked about friends. The Master said, "Faithfully admonish him, and kindly guide them. If this proves vain, stop. Do not disgrace yourself."

[原文] **12·24** 曾子曰:"君子以文会友,以友辅仁。"

[译文] 曾子说:"君子用文章学问来聚会朋友,凭借朋友来帮助自己培养仁德。"

Zeng Zi said, "A superior man gathers friends on literary grounds, and props his virtue by their friendship."

子路篇第十三

[原文]

13·1 子路问政。子曰:"先之劳之。"请益。曰:"无倦。"

[译文]

子路问怎样治理国家。孔子说:"凡事身先下属,身体力行,然后让他们勤劳地工作。"子路请求多讲一点。孔子说:"做事不要懈怠。"

Zilu asked about government. The Master said, "Take the lead and be laborious in their affairs. "Zilu requested further instruction, and was answered, "Never be weary in these things. "

[原文]

13·2 仲弓为季氏宰,问政。子曰:"先有司,赦小过,举贤才。"

曰:"焉知贤才而举之?"子曰:"举尔所知;尔所不知,人其舍诸?"

[译文]

仲弓做季氏的总管,问怎样管理政务。孔子说:"给有关工作人员带头,不计较人家小的过失,推荐优秀人才。"

仲弓说:"怎么知道谁是优秀人才而加以推举呢?"孔子说:"推举你所知道的。你所不知道的,别人难道会把他埋没吗?"

Zhonggong, being steward of the Ji family, asked about government. The Master said, "Let officers act first, pardon small faults, and promote men of virtue and talents. "

Zhonggong said, "How shall I know men of virtue and talents I have to promote?" The Master said, "Promote those you know. As to those you do not know, will others neglect them?"

[原文] **13·3** 子路曰:“卫君待子而为政,子将奚先?”

子曰:“必也正名乎!”

子路曰:“有是哉,子之迂也!奚其正?”

子曰:“野哉,由也!君子于其所不知,盖阙如也。名不正,则言不顺;言不顺,则事不成;事不成,则礼乐不兴;礼乐不兴,则刑罚不中;刑罚不中,则民无所措手足。故君子名之必可言也,言之必可行也。君子于其言,无所苟而已矣。”

[译文] 子路说:“卫国君主等待您去治理国政,您首先干什么呢?”

孔子说:“一定纠正名分上的用词不当吧!”

子路说:“您竟迂腐到这种程度啊!这有什么纠正的必要呢?”

孔子说:“仲由,真粗鲁!君子对他所不知道的只存疑在心中。用词不当,言语便不能顺理成章;言语不顺理成章,事情就办不好;事情办不好,国家的礼乐教化也就兴办不起来;礼乐教化兴办不起来,刑罚也就不会得当;刑罚不得当,老百姓就会不知如何是好。所以,君子用一个词,一定有其理由可以说得出来,顺理成章的话也一定可以行得通。君子对于措词说话,没有一点马虎的地方才罢了。”

Zilu said, “The prince of Wei has been waiting for you to govern. What shall you do first?”

The Master replied, “The one thing needed first is the rectification of names.”

“Indeed !” said Zilu, “You are getting so pedantic, Sir ! Why must rectify names?”

The Master said, “Zhong You, how crude you are! On matters that he does not know, a superior man shows a cautious reserve. If names are not right, what is said does not accord with the truth. When what is said does not accord with the truth, affairs cannot be carried on to success. When affairs cannot be carried on to success, rites and music do not flourish. When rites and music do not flourish, law and justice fail. And when law and justice fail, the people do not know how to move hand or foot. So a superior man consider it necessary that the names he uses may be spoken appropriately, and also that what he speaks may be carried out appropriately. The superior man, in what he says, leaves nothing to mere chance."

[原文] **13·4** 樊迟请学稼。子曰:"吾不如老农。"请学为圃。曰:"吾不如老圃。"

樊迟出。子曰:"小人哉,樊须也!上好礼,则民莫敢不敬;上好义,则民莫敢不服;上好信,则民莫敢不用情。夫如是,则四方之民襁负其子而至矣,焉用稼?"

[译文] 樊迟请教种庄稼。孔子说:"我赶不上老农民。"他又请教种菜蔬。孔子说:"我赶不上老菜农。"

樊迟退了出来。孔子说:"樊迟真是个小人!在上的人讲究礼节,百姓就没有人敢不敬重的;在上的人讲究情义,百姓就没有人敢不服从的;在上的人讲究诚信,百姓就没有人敢不说真话的。做到这样,四方的百姓都会背负着孩子来投奔你,哪里用得着自己种庄稼呢?"

Fan Chi asked to be taught farming. The Master said, "I am not so good at that as an old farmer." he asked to be taught gardening. The Master said, "I am not so good at that as an old gardener."

When Fan Chi left, the Master said, "A small man, indeed, is Fan Chi! If those above love propriety, the people will not dare to respect them; if those above love righteousness, the people will not dare to disobey; if those above love good faith, the people will not dare to hide the heart. Then, the people from all corners will come to him, bearing their children on their backs. What need will there be for farming?"

[原文] **13·5** 子曰:"诵《诗》三百,授之以政,不达;使于四方,不能专对;虽多,亦奚以为?"

[译文] 孔子说:"读了《诗经》三百篇,把政务交给他,完成不了;叫他出国办外交,又不能独立应对。这样,即使诗读得多,又有什么用处呢?"

The Master said, "Though a man may be able to recite the three hundred poems in the Book of Poetry, yet if, he does not know how to act when put to govern; if, he cannot answer for himself when sent on a mission to other states; despite the extent of his learning, of what use is it to him?"

[原文] **13·6** 子曰:"其身正,不令而行;其身不正,虽令不从。"

[译文] 孔子说:"本人正派,不发命令,事情也行得通。本人不正派,下达命令,别人也不会信从。"

The Master said, "When a ruler's personal conduct is correct, his government is effective without giving orders. If his personal conduct is not correct, even he may give orders, but they will not be followed."

[原文] 13·7 子曰:"鲁、卫之政,兄弟也。"

[译文] 孔子说:"鲁国、卫国的政治,像兄弟一样相差不远。"

The Master said, "In their politics Lu and Wei are brothers."

[原文] 13·8 子谓卫公子荆:"善居室。始有,曰:'苟合矣。'少有,曰:'苟完矣。'富有,曰:'苟美矣。'"

[译文] 孔子谈到卫国的公子荆,说:"他善于居家过日子,刚有一点家业,便说:'差不多够用了。'稍稍增加一些,便说:'差不多完备了。'相当富足了,便说:'差不多富丽堂皇了。'"

Speaking of grandee Jing of the Wei State, the Master said, "He knew the economy of a family well, when he began to have means, he said, 'This is much.' When he grew better off, he said, 'This is fairly complete.' And when he was rich, he said, 'We live in splendor.'"

[原文] 13·9 子适卫,冉有仆。子曰:"庶矣哉!"

冉有曰:"既庶矣,又何加焉?"曰:"富之。"

曰:"既富矣,又何加焉?"曰:"教之。"

[译文] 孔子到卫国去,冉有给他驾车。孔子说:"卫国人口好多呀!"

冉有说:"人口多了,又该干什么呢?"孔子说:"让他们富足。"

冉有又说:"他们富足了,又该干什么呢?"孔子说:"教育他们。"

When the Master went to Wei, Ran You drove the carriage for him. The Master said, "What a dense population!"

Ran You said, "Since the people are already numerous, What next should be done for them?" The Master said, "Enrich them."

"And when they have been enriched, what next should be done for them?" The Master said, "Teach them."

[原文] **13·10** 子曰:"苟有用我者,期月而已可也,三年有成。"

[译文] 孔子说:"假如有人要我主持国家政事,一年可以初见成效,三年会大见成效。"

The Master said, "If I were employed in the government, in twelve months, all would win initial success. In three years, all would achieve remarkable success."

[原文] **13·11** 子曰:"'善人为邦百年,亦可以胜残去杀矣。'诚哉是言也!"

[译文] 孔子说:"'好人治理国家,连续一百年,也可以克服残暴,免除虐杀了。'这句话说得真对呀!"

The Master said, "'If good men were to govern a country for a hundred years, it would be really possible to stop cruelty and do away with slaughter.' True indeed is this saying!"

[原文] **13·12** 子曰:"如有王者,必世而后仁。"

[译文] 孔子说:"如果有以德服人的圣君出现,也要经过三十年,才能实行仁政。"

The Master said, "If a truly royal ruler were to arise, within thirty years virtue would prevail."

[原文] **13·13** 子曰:“苟正其身矣,于从政乎何有?不能正其身,如正人何?”

[译文] 孔子说:“如果自身端正了,对治理国政有什么困难呢?连本身都不能端正,怎样能端正别人呢?”

The Master said, “If a ruler makes his own conduct correct, what difficulty will he have in governing? If he cannot rectify himself, what has he to do with rectifying others?”

[原文] **13·14** 冉子退朝。子曰:“何晏也?”对曰:“有政。”子曰:“其事也。如有政,虽不吾以,吾其与闻之。”

[译文] 冉有从公廷回来。孔子说:“为什么回来这么晚?”冉有回答说:“有政务要办。”孔子说:“那只是事务罢了。假若有政务要办,虽然不用我,我也会知道。”

As the disciple Ran You came back from the court, the Master said to him, “Why are you so late?” he answered, “I had government affairs.” The Master said, “It must have been general affairs. If there had been government affairs, though I am not used, I should have been heard of it.”

[原文] **13·15** 定公问:“一言而可以兴邦,有诸?”

孔子对曰:“言不可以若是其几也。人之言曰:‘为君难,为臣不易。’如知为君之难也,不几乎一言而兴邦乎?”

曰:“一言而丧邦,有诸?”

孔子对曰:“言不可以若是其几也。人之言曰:

'予无乐乎为君,唯其言而莫予违也。'如其善而莫之违也,不亦善乎? 如不善而莫之违也,不几乎一言而丧邦乎?"

[译文] 鲁定公问:"一句话可以使国家兴盛,有这回事吗?"

孔子回答说:"话不能说得这样简单。有人说:'做国君难,做臣子也不容易。'如果知道做国君的艰难,不是近乎一句话便能使国家兴盛吗?"

鲁定公又问:"一句话可以丧失国家,有这回事么?"

孔子回答说:"话不能说得这样简单。有人说:'我做国君没有别的乐趣,唯一高兴的是我说话没有人违抗。'假若说的话正确而没有人违抗,不也好吗? 假若说得不正确,也没有人违抗,不是近于一句话就可以丧失国家吗?"

Duke Ding asked, "Is there any one saying that can make a state prosperous?"

Confucius answered, "It cannot be said so simply. However, there is a saying which people have, 'To be a prince is difficult, to be a minister is not easy.' And does one know how difficult it is to be a prince, might not this one saying all but make a state prosperous?"

The duke said, "Is there any one saying that can ruin a state?"

Confucius answered, "It cannot be said so simply. However, there is a saying which people have, 'I have no pleasure in being a prince, only in that no one opposes what I say.' If a prince's words are right, and no one opposes them, is it not good? But if they are not right, and no one opposes them, might not this one saying all but ruin a state?"

[原文] **13·16 叶公问政。子曰:“近者悦,远者来。”**

[译文] 叶公问怎样管理政事。孔子说:“让近处的人感到高兴,让远方的人来投奔你。”

The Duke of She asked about government. The Master said, “To gladden those around you and attract men from afar.”

[原文] **13·17 子夏为莒父宰,问政。子曰:“无欲速,无见小利。欲速,则不达;见小利,则大事不成。”**

[译文] 子夏做莒父的县长,问怎样治理。孔子说:“不要急于求成,不要顾及小利益。想要快,就反而不能达到预期的目的;顾及小利益,就办不成大事。”

Zixia, being governor of Jufu, asked about government. The Master said, “Do not desire to have things done quickly; do not covert small advantages. Desire to have things done quickly prevents their being done thoroughly. Coverting small advantages prevents important things from being accomplished.”

[原文] **13·18 叶公语孔子曰:“吾党有直躬者,其父攘羊,而子证之。”孔子曰:“吾党之直者异于是:父为子隐,子为父隐,直在其中矣。”**

[译文] 叶公告诉孔子说:“我那里有个坦白直率的人,他父亲偷了羊,这儿子便去告发。”孔子说:“我家乡坦白直率的人和这不同,父亲替儿子隐瞒,儿子替父亲隐瞒,坦白直率就包含在这里面了。”

The Duke of She told Confucius, “In my hometown there is an upright man. His father stole a sheep, he born witness against him.” Confucius said, “In my hometown, the people’s uprightness is unlike that. The father screens his son, the son screens his father. Uprightness is in this."

[原文] **13·19** 樊迟问仁。子曰:"居处恭,执事敬,与人忠。虽之夷狄,不可弃也。"

[译文] 樊迟问什么是仁。孔子说:"平日在家容貌态度端庄,办事情严肃认真,为别人做事诚心实意。这几种品德,即使到夷狄地区也是不可抛弃的。"

Fan Chi asked about perfect virtue. The Master said, "To be respectful at home, painstaking at work, faithful to all. Even among rude uncultivated tribes, none of this may be dropped."

[原文] **13·20** 子贡问曰:"何如斯可谓之士矣?"子曰:"行己有耻,使于四方,不辱君命,可谓士矣。"

曰:"敢问其次。"曰:"宗族称孝焉,乡党称弟焉。"

曰:"敢问其次。"曰:"言必信,行必果,硁硁然小人哉! 抑亦可以为次矣。"

曰:"今之从政者何如?"子曰:"噫! 斗筲之人,何足算也?"

[译文] 子贡问:"怎样才能叫'士'呢?"孔子说:"自己行事知道羞耻,出使外国能很好完成国君交给的使命,可以叫做'士'了。"

子贡问:"请问次一等的呢?"孔子说:"本宗族的人称赞他孝顺父母,本乡本地的人称赞他尊敬长者。"

子贡又问:"再次一等的呢?"孔子说:"说话一定讲信用,做事一定果断,这是不问是非曲直只求贯彻自己言行的小人呀,但也可以说是再次一等的'士'了。"

子贡又问:"现在这些在位的人怎样?"孔子说:"唉! 胸

襟狭小的人,算得了什么呀?"

Zigong asked, "What qualities must a man possess to be called a superior man?" The Master said, "He who maintains a sense of shame in his personal conduct; and when sent to any state does not disgrace his prince's commission, may be called a superior man."

Zigong said, "May I ask who would rank next?" The Master said, "The man whom his clansmen praised for his filial piety, his villagers praised for his respect to the elders."

Again Zigong asked, "May I ask who would rank next?" The Master said, "He who is determined to do what he says, and to carry out what he does, never minds they are right or not, a obstinate small man, yet perhaps would come next."

Zigong asked, "How are those who engage in government today?" The Master said, "Pooh! These narrow-minded small men, not worth being taken into account."

[原文] **13·21** 子曰:"不得中行而与之,必也狂狷乎!狂者进取,狷者有所不为也。"

[译文] 孔子说:"不能与言行中庸的人交往,那只有和激进的人或洁身自好的人相交吧!激进的人勇于进取,洁身自好的人不去干坏事。"

The Master said, "Since I cannot get men pursuing the golden mean to communicate with, I must find the ardent and the cautiously-decided. The ardent will press forward, the cautiously-decided will keep themselves from what is wrong."

[原文] **13·22** 子曰:“南人有言曰:‘人而无恒,不可以作巫医。’善夫!”

“不恒其德,或承之羞。”子曰:“不占而已矣。”

[译文] 孔子说:“南方人有句话:‘人如果没有恒心,连巫医都做不了。’这话真好呀!”

《易经》说:“不长期坚守自己的道德,总有人招致羞辱。”孔子又说:“这是叫无恒心的人不必去占卦。”

The Master said, “The people of the south have a saying—‘A man without constancy even cannot make a wizard-doctor.’ Well said !”

The Books of Change says “Inconstant in his virtue, he will incur disgrace.” The Master said, “What this sentence means is that those without constancy need not go to divine.”

[原文] **13·23** 子曰:“君子和而不同,小人同而不和。”

[译文] 孔子说:“君子讲究互相协调,而不盲目随从;小人则盲目随从,而不讲究协调。”

The Master said, “The superior man is conciliatory but not blind-accommodating; the small man is blind-accommodating but not conciliatory.”

[原文] **13·24** 子贡问曰:“乡人皆好之,何如?”子曰:“未可也。”

“乡人皆恶之,何如?”子曰:“未可也;不如乡人之善者好之,其不善者恶之。”

[译文] 子贡问道:“一乡的人都喜欢他,这人怎么样?”孔子说:“不一定好。”

子贡又问:“一乡的人都厌恶他,这人怎么样?”孔子说:“不一定坏。最好是一乡的好人喜欢他,坏人厌恶他。”

Zigong asked, “What do you say of a man who is loved by all his fellow-villagers?” The Master said, “That is not enough.”

“And what do you say of a man who is hated by all his fellow-villagers?” The Master said, “That is not enough. Best of all would be that the good in the village love him and the bad hate him.”

[原文] **13·25 子曰:“君子易事而难说也。说之不以道,不说也;及其使人也,器之。小人难事而易说也。说之虽不以道,说也;及其使人也,求备焉。”**

[译文] 孔子说:“在君子手下工作容易,讨他的欢喜却难。不用正当的方式去讨他喜欢,他是不会喜欢的;等到他使唤人的时候,衡量各人的才德去分配任务。在小人手下工作难,讨他喜欢却容易。用不正当的方式讨他喜欢,他也会喜欢,等到他使唤人的时候,便百般挑剔,求全责备。”

The Master said, “A superior man is easy to serve and difficult to please. If you try to please him in any manner which is not accordant with the Way, he will not be pleased. But in his employment of men, he uses them according to their capacity. The small man is difficult to serve and easy to please. If you try to please him, even though in a manner which is not accordant with the Way, he will be pleased. But in his employment of men, he expects them to do any work that comes along.”

[原文] **13·26 子曰:“君子泰而不骄,小人骄而不泰。”**

[译文] 孔子说："君子安详舒展，而不傲慢；小人傲慢，而不安详舒展。"

The Master said, "The superior man has dignified ease, but without pride; the small man has pride, but without dignified ease."

[原文] **13·27 子曰："刚、毅、木、讷近仁。"**

[译文] 孔子说："刚强、果断、质朴、言语谨慎，具有这四种品德的人接近于仁。"

The Master said, "Fortitude, resolution, simplicity and caution in speech are near to the perfect virtue."

[原文] **13·28 子路问曰："何如斯可谓之士矣？"子曰："切切偲偲，怡怡如也，可谓士矣。朋友切切偲偲，兄弟怡怡。"**

[译文] 子路问道："怎样才可以称作'士'？"孔子说："互相恳切地批评勉励，和睦共处，可以称作'士'了。朋友之间，应互相恳切地批评勉励，兄弟之间应和睦共处。"

Zilu asked, "What qualities must a man possess to be called a superior man?" The Master said, "A man who is earnest and encouraging, kind and bland may be called a superior man. Among his friends, earnest and encouraging; among his brothers, kind and bland."

[原文] **13·29 子曰："善人教民七年，亦可以即戎矣。"**

[译文] 孔子说："善人教导人民七年，也可以叫他们去作战了。"

The Master said, "Could a good man instruct the people for

seven years, they would be fit for arms also."

[原文] **13·30** 子曰:"以不教民战,是谓弃之。"

[译文] 孔子说:"用没有受过军事训练的人民去作战,这叫做抛弃他们。"

The Master said, "To lead untrained men into war, is to throw them away."

宪问篇第十四

[原文] **14·1** 宪问耻。子曰:“邦有道,谷;邦无道,谷,耻也。”

“克、伐、怨、欲不行焉,可以为仁矣?”子曰:“可以为难矣,仁则吾不知也。”

[译文] 原宪问什么是耻辱。孔子说:“国家政治清平,做官拿俸谷;国家腐败黑暗,做官也拿俸谷,这就是耻辱。”

原宪又说:“好胜、自夸、怨恨和贪心都没有表现过,可以说是仁了吧?”孔子说:“可以说是难能可贵了,是否仁,我不知道。”

Yuan Xuan① asked what was shameful. The Master said, “When the Way prevails in the state, to take office and accept salary; and when the Way does not prevail in the state, still to take office and accept salary, this is shameful.”

“To eschew the love of mastery, boasting, resentment and greed, can that be called perfect virtue?” The Master said, “That may be called what is difficult to do, but whether it should be called perfect virtue I do not know.”

[注释] ① i. e. Yuan Si.

[原文] **14·2** 子曰:“士而怀居,不足以为士矣。”

[译文] 孔子说:“士如果留恋安逸生活,便不足以成为士了。”

The Master said, “The superior man who cherishes only the love of comfort is not worthy the name.”

[原文] **14·3** 子曰:“邦有道,危言危行;邦无道,危行言孙。”

[译文] 孔子说:“国家政治清平,说话正直,行为正直;国家腐败黑暗,行为正直,说话谦顺。”

The Master said, “When the Way prevails in the state, be upright in speech and upright in action; when the Way does not prevail, be upright in action but modest in speech.”

[原文] **14·4** 子曰:“有德者必有言,有言者不必有德。仁者必有勇,勇者不必有仁。”

[译文] 孔子说:“有道德的人一定有名言;有名言的人却不一定有道德。仁德的人一定勇敢,勇敢的人却不一定有仁德。”

The Master said, “A man of virtue will be sure to possess eloquence, but those who possess eloquence may not always be men of virtue. A man of human-heartedness will be sure to possess courage, but those who possess courage may not always be men of human-heartedness.”

[原文] **14·5** 南宫适问于孔子曰:“羿善射,奡荡舟,俱不得其死然。禹稷躬稼而有天下。”夫子不答。

南宫适出,子曰:“君子哉若人!尚德哉若人!”

[译文] 南宫适问孔子说:“羿擅长射箭,奡擅长水战,都没有得到好死。禹和稷亲自下地种田,得到了天下。”孔子没有回答。

南宫适出来后,孔子说:“这个人是个君子啊!这个人多么崇尚道德啊!”

Nangong Kuo said to Confucius, “Yi was good at archery, Ao could move a boat overland, but neither of them died a natural death. Yu and Ji personally toiled at their crops and won the world." The Master made no reply.

But when Nangong Kuo went out, the Master said, "What a superior man he is! How he prizes virtue!"

[原文] **14·6** 子曰："君子而不仁者有矣夫，未有小人而仁者也。"

[译文] 孔子说："君子当中有不仁德的人吧，小人当中却不会有仁德的人。"

The Master said, "Superior men, and yet without human-heartedness, there may be. But there never has been a small man with human-heartedness."

[原文] **14·7** 子曰："爱之，能勿劳乎？忠焉，能勿诲乎？"

[译文] 孔子说："爱他，能够不让他劳累吗？对他效忠竭力，能够不教诲他吗？"

The Master said, "Can there be love which does not lead to the toil of its object? Can there be loyalty which does not lead to the instruction of its object?"

[原文] **14·8** 子曰："为命，裨谌草创之，世叔讨论之，行人子羽修饰之，东里子产润色之。"

[译文] 孔子说："郑国的法令文件，由裨谌拟稿，世叔提意见，外交官子羽修改润饰，东里的子产作文辞上的加工。"

The Master said, "In preparing the decrees, Bi Chen first made the rough draft; Shishu checked and revised it; Ziyu, the manager of foreign affairs, amended it; and Zichan of Dong Li polished it and gave it the proper elegance."

[原文] 14·9 或问子产。子曰:"惠人也。"

问子西。曰:"彼哉!彼哉!"

问管仲。曰:"人也。夺伯氏骈邑三百,饭疏食,没齿无怨言。"

[译文] 有人问子产怎么样。孔子说:"是位仁慈恩惠的人。"

又问子西怎么样。孔子说:"他呀,他呀!"

又问到管仲怎么样。孔子说:"是个人才。他剥夺了伯氏封地三百户的骈邑,自己只吃粗粮,到死没有一句怨恨的话。"

Someone asked about Zichan. The Master said, "He was a kind-hearted man."

He asked about Zixi. The Master said, "That man! That man!"

Asked about Guang Zhong, the Master said, "He was the man of ability. He took the town of Pian with its three hundred households from its owner Bo; yet Bo, though he had only coarse rice to eat till his death, could find no word of resentment to say."

[原文] 14·10 子曰:"贫而无怨难,富而无骄易。"

[译文] 孔子说:"贫困却没有怨恨是很难的,富贵却不骄傲是容易的。"

The Master said, "To be poor without resentment is difficult; to be rich without being proud is easier."

[原文] 14·11 子曰:"孟公绰为赵、魏老则优,不可以

为滕、薛大夫。”

［译文］ 孔子说：“孟公绰做晋国大臣赵家、魏家的总管，能力有余，却不能做滕、薛这样小国的大夫。”

The Master said, “Meng Gongchuo is more than fit to be steward to the Zhao and Wei families, but he is not fit to be minister of either Teng or Xue State.”

［原文］ **14·12 子路问成人。子曰：“若臧武仲之知，公绰之不欲，卞庄子之勇，冉求之艺，文之以礼乐，亦可以为成人矣。”曰：“今之成人者何必然？见利思义，见危授命，久要不忘平生之言，亦可以为成人矣。”**

［译文］ 子路问怎么样才是一个完美无缺的人。孔子说：“聪明智慧像臧武仲，清心寡欲像孟公绰，勇敢像卞庄子，多才多艺像冉求，再用礼乐来增加他的文采，可以说是完美无缺的人了。”又说：“现在完美无缺的人哪里一定要这样，看见利益能想到道义，碰到危险愿献出生命，长期穷困而不忘记平日的诺言，这样也可以说是完美无缺的人了。”

Zilu asked what was meant by ‘a perfect man’. The Master said, “A man wise as Zang Wuzhong, uncovetous as Meng Gongchuo, bold as Bian Zhuang Zi, gifted as Ran Qiu, and graced with the rules of propriety and music, might be called a perfect man.” He then added, “But today who asks all these of a perfect man? The man, who in sight of gain remembers righteousness, in face of danger will risk his life, in the longstanding poverty will cleave to his promise, may be called a perfect man.”

[原文] **14·13** 子问公叔文子于公明贾曰:"信乎,夫子不言,不笑,不取乎?"

公明贾对曰:"以告者过也。夫子时然后言,人不厌其言;乐然后笑,人不厌其笑;义然后取,人不厌其取。"

子曰:"其然?岂其然乎?"

[译文] 孔子向公明贾问到公叔文子,说:"他老人家不说话,不笑,不贪取,是真的吗?"

公明贾回答说:"这是告诉您的人说错了。他老人家该说时才说,别人不厌恶他的话;高兴了才笑,别人不讨厌他的笑;合乎情理应该取的才取,别人不厌恶他的取。"

孔子说:"是这样吗?难道真的是这样吗?"

The Master asked Gongming Jia about Gongshu Wen Zi, saying, "Is it true that he does not speak, nor laugh, nor take?"

Gongming Jia replied, "The man who told you this was exaggerating. The Master speaks when it is the time to speak, so none is weary of his speaking; he laughs when he is joyful, so none is weary of his laughter; he takes what is right to take, so none is weary of his taking."

The Master said, "Was that so? Can that really have been so?"

[原文] **14·14** 子曰:"臧武仲以防求为后于鲁,虽曰不要君,吾不信也。"

[译文] 孔子说:"臧武仲凭借他的封地防城,向鲁君要求立他的后人为卿大夫,虽说不是要挟国君,我却不相信。"

The Master said, "Zang Wuzhong, holding the fief of Fang,

asked the prince of Lu to appoint his descendants as senior officials in Lu. Though it was said that he was not forcing his prince, I cannot believe it."

[原文] **14·15** 子曰："晋文公谲而不正，齐桓公正而不谲。"

[译文] 孔子说："晋文公诡诈而不正派；齐桓公正派而不诡诈。"

The Master said, "Duke Wen of Jin was crafty and not upright. Duke Huan of Qi was upright and not crafty."

[原文] **14·16** 子路曰："桓公杀公子纠，召忽死之，管仲不死。"曰："未仁乎?"子曰："桓公九合诸侯，不以兵车，管仲之力也。如其仁，如其仁。"

[译文] 子路说："齐桓公杀了公子纠，召忽也自杀了，管仲却不死。"又说："管仲可说是没有仁德吧?"孔子说："齐桓公多次聚集各国君主结盟，不用武力，都是管仲出的力。这就是他的仁德！这就是他的仁德!"

Zilu said, "When Duke Huan of Qi slew his brother grandee Jiu, Zhao Hu died with him, but Guan Zhong did not. Was he not want in virtue?" The Master said, "The Duke Huan was able to convene the princes of all the states without resorting to the use of weapons and chariots of war; it was all due to Guan Zhong. Such is his virtue ! Such is his virtue !"

[原文] **14·17** 子贡曰："管仲非仁者与？桓公杀公子纠，不能死，又相之。"子曰："管仲相桓公，霸诸侯，一匡天下，民到于今受其赐。微管仲，吾其被发左

衽矣。岂若匹夫匹妇之为谅也，自经于沟渎而莫之知也？”

[译文] 子贡说：“管仲不是一个有仁德的人吧？桓公杀了公子纠，管仲不自杀，又去辅佐齐桓公。”孔子说：“管子辅佐齐桓公，称霸诸侯，匡正天下，百姓到今天还蒙受他的好处。假使没有管仲，我们都会披散头发，衣襟向左边开，（沦为落后民族了。）他难道也要像普通人那样，守着小节小信在山沟中上吊自杀，而没有人知道吗？”

Zigong said, “Guan Zhong, I think, was not a man of virtue. When Duke Huan slew his brother Prince Jiu, Guan Zhong did not die with him, moreover he became prime minister to Huan.” The Master said, “By Guan Zhong's help, Duke Huan became leader of all the feudal princes, and united and rectified the whole world. Down to the present day the people have benefited from what he then did. But for Guan Zhong, we should now wear our hair dishevelled and fold our clothes to the left. Will you except from him the small fidelity of common men and common women, who would commit suicide in a stream or ditch, no one knowing about them?”

[原文] **14·18** 公叔文子之臣大夫僎与文子同升诸公。子闻之，曰：“可以为‘文’矣。”

[译文] 公叔文子的家臣大夫僎，由于文子向朝廷推荐他，和文子一同做了大臣。孔子听到这件事，说：“文子可以得到‘文’的谥号了。”

Gongshu Wen Zi became a minister of Wei together with his retainer Xun. When the Master heard of this, he said, “He deserves to be called Wen(cultured)."

[原文] **14·19** 子言卫灵公之无道也,康子曰:"夫如是,奚而不丧?"孔子曰:"仲叔圉治宾客,祝鮀治宗庙,王孙贾治军旅。夫如是,奚其丧?"

[译文] 孔子谈到卫灵公的昏庸无道,季康子说:"他既然这样,为什么没有灭亡呢?"孔子说:"他有仲叔圉接待宾客,祝鮀管理祭祀,王孙贾统率军队。像这样,怎么会灭亡?"

When the Master said that Duke Ling of Wei did not follow the right way, Ji Kang Zi asked, "Since he is like that, why has he not lost his throne?" Confucius answered, "He has Zhongshu Yu to deal with foreign envoys and guests, Zhu Tuo in charge of the ancestral temple, and Wangsun Jia to command the army, how should he lose his throne?"

[原文] **14·20** 子曰:"其言之不怍,则为之也难。"

[译文] 孔子说:"一个人大言不惭,他做起来就不容易。"

The Master said, "He who speaks without modesty will find it difficult to put his words into practice."

[原文] **14·21** 陈成子弑简公。孔子沐浴而朝,告于哀公曰:"陈恒弑其君,请讨之。"公曰:"告夫三子!"

孔子曰:"以吾从大夫之后,不敢不告也。君曰'告夫三子'者!"

之三子告,不可。孔子曰:"以吾从大夫之后,不敢不告也。"

[译文] 陈成子杀了齐简公。孔子沐浴斋戒后去上朝,报告鲁哀

公说:"陈恒杀了他的君主,请求您讨伐他。"鲁哀公说:"你告诉季孙、仲孙、孟孙三位大臣吧!"

孔子退朝后说:"我曾忝列大夫之官,不敢不报告,君主却说:'告诉那三位去吧!'"

孔子又到三位大夫那里去报告,三位大夫不同意。孔子说:"我曾忝列大夫之官,不敢不来报告。"

When Chen Cheng Zi murdered Duke Jian of Qi, Confucius bathed, went to court, and told Duke Ai, saying, "Chen Heng has slain his prince. Please dispatch troops to punish him." The duke said, "Inform the three chiefs."

Confucius said, "Following in the wake of the great officers, I dared not to leave such a matter untold. But the prince says, 'Inform the three chiefs.'"

He then informed the three chiefs. They refused to act. Confucius said, "Following in the wake of the great officers, I dared not to leave such a matter untold."

[原文] **14·22 子路问事君。子曰:"勿欺也,而犯之。"**

[译文] 子路问怎样服侍国君。孔子说:"不要欺骗,但可以当面直言触犯他。"

Zilu asked how to serve a prince. The Master said, "Never cheat him; withstand him to his face."

[原文] **14·23 子曰:"君子上达,小人下达。"**

[译文] 孔子说:"君子向上,通达仁义;小人向下,追求财利。"

The Master said, "A superior man has a complete understanding of righteousness; the small man has a complete understanding of profit."

[原文] **14·24** 子曰:"古之学者为己,今之学者为人。"

[译文] 孔子说:"古代人学习是为了提高自己,现在的人学习是为了给别人看。"

The Master said, "In ancient times men learned for the sake of self-improvement; nowadays men learn for show."

[原文] **14·25** 蘧伯玉使人于孔子。孔子与之坐而问焉,曰:"夫子何为?"对曰:"夫子欲寡其过而未能也。"

使者出。子曰:"使乎! 使乎!"

[译文] 蘧伯玉派一位使者去拜访孔子。孔子给他一个席位,问道:"他老人家干些什么?"使者回答说:"他老人家想要减少失误,却还没能做到。"

使者出来后。孔子说:"好一位使者! 好一位使者!"

Qu Boyu sent a messenger to Confucius. Confucius sat with him and asked, "What is the master doing?" The messenger replied, "He is trying to make his faults few, but he has not yet succeeded."

When the messenger had left, the Master said, "What a messenger! What a messenger!"

[原文] **14·26** 子曰:"不在其位,不谋其政。"

曾子曰:"君子思不出其位。"

[译文] 孔子说:"不在那个职位,不考虑那方面的政事。"

曾子说:"君子思考的问题不超越他的职务范围。"

The Master said, "He who is not in any particular office does not discuss its policies."

Zeng Zi said, "The superior man does not think of more than his own duties."

［原文］ **14·27** 子曰："君子耻其言而过其行。"

［译文］ 孔子说："君子认为所说的超过了所做的是可耻的。"

The Master said, "The superior man is ashamed to speak more and do less."

［原文］ **14·28** 子曰："君子道者三，我无能焉：仁者不忧，知者不惑，勇者不惧。"子贡曰："夫子自道也。"

［译文］ 孔子说："君子为人要做的有三件，我没有做到：仁德的人不忧愁，智慧的人不迷惑，勇敢的人不畏惧。"子贡说："这正是老师的自我表述。"

The Master said, "The ways of the superior man are three, but I have met with success in none of them. The virtuous is free from anxieties; the wise is free from doubts; the bold is free from fear." Zigong said, "That is what our master say about himself."

［原文］ **14·29** 子贡方人。子曰："赐也贤乎哉？夫我则不暇。"

［译文］ 子贡评论别人。孔子说："端木赐，你就够好了吗？我就没有这闲工夫。"

Zigong was criticizing other people. The Master said, "Have you been perfect yourself? I myself have no time for this."

[原文] **14·30** 子曰:“不患人之不己知,患其不能也。”

[译文] 孔子说:“不担心别人不知道自己,只担心自己没有能力。”

The Master said, “I'm not concerned at men's not knowing me. I'm concerned at my own want of ability.”

[原文] **14·31** 子曰:“不逆诈,不億不信,抑亦先觉者,是贤乎!”

[译文] 孔子说:“不预先怀疑别人欺诈,也不无根据地猜测别人不老实,却能及早察觉出来,这是位贤者吧!”

The Master said, “He who does not doubt about others'deceit, nor harbors a groundless suspicion against their dishonesty, and yet can apprehend these things readily; —is he not a man of worth?”

[原文] **14·32** 微生亩谓孔子曰:“丘何为是栖栖者与?无乃为佞乎?”孔子曰:“非敢为佞也,疾固也。”

[译文] 微生亩对孔子说:“你为什么这样忙忙碌碌呢? 不是成了能言善辩的人吗?”孔子说:“我不敢成为能言善辩的人,而是痛恨那种顽固不化的人。”

Weisheng Mu said to Confucius, “Why are you so busy? Are you not wagging a glib tongue?” Confucius answered, “I dare not wag a glib tongue, but I hate stubbornness.”

[原文] **14·33** 子曰:“骥不称其力,称其德也。”

[译文] 孔子说:“称千里马叫骥,不是赞美它的力气,而是赞美它的品德。”

The Master said, “A steed is not praised for its strength, but praised for its good qualities."

[原文] **14·34** 或曰:"以德报怨,何如?"子曰:"何以报德?以直报怨,以德报德。"

[译文] 有人说:"用恩德来报答怨恨,怎么样?"孔子说:"那你用什么来报答恩德呢?应该用正直来报答怨恨,用恩德来报答恩德。"

Someone said, "To requite resentment with kindness, what do you think of that?" The Master said, "With what then will you requite kindness? Requite resentment with justice; requite kindness with kindness."

[原文] **14·35** 子曰:"莫我知也夫!"子贡曰:"何为其莫知子也?"子曰:"不怨天,不尤人,下学而上达。知我者其天乎!"

[译文] 孔子说:"没有人知道我呀!"子贡说:"为什么没有人知道您呢?"孔子说:"不怨恨上天,不责备别人,学习平常知识,透彻了解高深的道理。知道我的只是上天吧!"

The Master said, "Alas! no one knows me!" Zigong asked, "Why do you say that no one knows you?" The Master replied, "I do not accuse Heaven, nor do I lay the blame on men. My studies lie low, and my penetration rises high. I am known but to Heaven!"

[原文] **14·36** 公伯寮愬子路于季孙。子服景伯以告,曰:"夫子固有惑志于公伯寮,吾力犹能肆诸市朝。"

子曰："道之将行也与，命也；道之将废也与，命也。公伯寮其如命何！"

[译文] 公伯寮在季孙氏面前毁谤子路。子服景伯告诉孔子，说："他老人家已经被公伯寮迷惑了，我还有力量杀了他陈尸街头示众。"

孔子说："我的主张将要实行，是命运决定；我的主张将被废除，也决定于命运。公伯寮又能把命运怎么样呢！"

Gongbo Liao spoke ill of Zilu to Jisun. Zifu Jingbo told this to Confucius, saying, "The old man's mind is surely being led astray by Gongbo Liao, but I still have enough strength to expose his corpse in the market."

The Master said, "If my principles are to prevail in the world, it is the will of Heaven. If they are to fall to the ground, it is also the will of Heaven. Can Gongbo Liao fight against the will of Heaven?"

[原文] **14·37** 子曰："贤者辟世，其次辟地，其次辟色，其次辟言。"

子曰："作者七人矣。"

[译文] 孔子说："贤能的人逃避恶浊社会而隐居，次一等的人躲开最坏的地方择地而处，再次一等的人避开某些人难看的脸色，再次一等的人避开恶言恶语。"

孔子说："这样做的已经有七人了。"

The Master said, "Men of worth shun the world; the next best shun the land; then come men who go at a look, then men who go at a word."

The Master said, "Seven men did so."

[原文] **14·38** 子路宿于石门。晨门曰:“奚自?”子路曰:“自孔氏。”曰:“是知其不可而为之者与?”

[译文] 子路在石门住了一夜,(第二天清早进城,)早上管城门的人问:“从哪里来?”子路说:“从孔家来。”那人说:“是那个明知做不到却偏要做的人吗?”

Zilu spent a night at Shimen. The gate-keeper asked him, “Where do you come from?” Zi Lu said, “From Master Kong's.” “The man knows that he cannot succeed, yet keeps on trying to do it?” said the gate-keeper.

[原文] **14·39** 子击磬于卫,有荷蒉而过孔氏之门者,曰:“有心哉,击磬乎!”既而曰:“鄙哉,硁硁乎!莫己知也,斯己而已矣。深则厉,浅则揭。”

子曰:“果哉!末之难矣。”

[译文] 孔子在卫国有一天敲着磬,有个挑草筐的人在门前走过,说:“敲磬的是位有心人呀!”过一会儿又说:“磬声硁硁的,真鄙俗呀!(它好像在说没有人知道我啊!)没有人知道自己,这就算了。水深就把衣裳脱下来,水浅就撩起裙子。”

孔子说:“好坚决,没有办法说服他了。”

One day when the Master was playing Qing① in Wei, a man, carrying a straw basket, passed the door and said, “His heart is full, who so plays Qing!” A moment later, he added, “For shame! What a tinkling note ! If no one knows you, you can just do things for yourself. When the water is deep, cross it with clothes on; when it is shallow, cross it with the clothes held up.” The Master said, “How determined is he in his purpose! It is impossible to persuade him.”

[注释] ① A kind of musical instrument made of stone.

[原文] **14·40** 子张曰："《书》云：'高宗谅阴，三年不言。'何谓也？"子曰："何必高宗，古之人皆然。君薨，百官总己以听于冢宰三年。"

[译文] 子张说："《尚书》说：'殷高宗守孝，住在凶庐，三年不讲话。'这是什么意思？"孔子说："哪里一定是高宗，古代人都这样。国君死了，继承君位的人三年不谈政事，各部门官员自理政务而听命于宰相。"

Zizhang said, "The Book of History says, 'Gaozong[①], when mourning his father, did not speak for three years.' What does this mean?" The Master said, "Not Gaozong in particular. The ancients all did so. Whenever a prince died, the ministers all continued in their offices, taking their orders from the Prime Minister for three years."

[注释] ① The King of the Shang dynasty.

[原文] **14·41** 子曰："上好礼，则民易使也。"

[译文] 孔子说："在上位的人讲究礼法，依礼而行，百姓就容易使唤。"

The Master said, "When rulers love the rules of propriety, the people are easy to lead."

[原文] **14·42** 子路问君子。子曰："修己以敬。"

曰："如斯而已乎？"曰："修己以安人。"

曰："如斯而已乎？"曰："修己以安百姓。修己以安百姓，尧、舜其犹病诸？"

[译文] 子路问怎样才是君子。孔子说："修养自己，恭敬谨慎。"

子路说:"这样就够了吗?"孔子说:"修养自己,使亲友安乐。"

子路说:"这样就够了吗?"孔子说:"修养自己,使百姓安乐。修养自己,使百姓安乐,可能尧、舜还做不到呢!"

Zilu asked what constituted a superior man. The Master said, "A man who cultivates in himself the capacity to be diligent in his tasks."

"And is this all?" said Zilu. "He cultivates himself to give ease to others."

"And is that all?" "He cultivates himself to give ease to all the people," said the Master, "To cultivate himself to give ease to all the people, —even Yao and Shun still found it difficult."

[原文] **14·43** 原壤夷俟。子曰:"幼而不孙弟,长而无述焉,老而不死,是为贼。"以杖叩其胫。

[译文] 原壤撇着两腿坐着等孔子。孔子说:"你小时候不孝不悌,长大了毫无贡献,老了还不死,真是个害人精。"然后用拐杖敲他小腿。

Yuan Rang① sat waiting for the Master in a sprawling position. The Master said, "You did not know the rules of propriety when young, and achieved nothing as adult. You merely live on, getting older and older. A pest indeed!" With this he hit him on the leg with his staff.

[注释] ① A friend of Confucius.

[原文] **14·44** 阙党童子将命。或问之曰:"益者与?"子曰:"吾见其居于位也,见其与先生并行也。非求益者也,欲速成者也。"

[译文] 阙党地方的一个童子来向孔子传话。有人问孔子说:“他是求上进的人吗?”孔子说:“我看见他坐在成年人的席位上,又看见他同长辈并肩而行。这人不是肯求上进的人,而是急于求成的人。”

When a boy from the village of Que was made message-bearer, someone asked, “Is he improving himself?” The Master said, “I see him sitting in the seat of a grown-up man, see him walking shoulder to shoulder with his elders. He is not one who wishes to improve himself. He was only overanxious for quick results.”

卫灵公篇第十五

［原文］

15·1 卫灵公问陈于孔子。孔子对曰："俎豆之事，则尝闻之矣；军旅之事，未之学也。"明日遂行。

［译文］

卫灵公向孔子询问作战的阵势。孔子回答说："礼仪的事情，曾经听说过；军队作战的事情，我没有学习过。"于是第二天离开卫国。

Duke Ling of Wei asked Confucius about tactics. Confucius replied, "Of sacrificial rites I have learned, but I have never studied military matters." Next day he left.

［原文］

15·2 在陈绝粮，从者病，莫能兴。子路愠见曰："君子亦有穷乎？"子曰："君子固穷，小人穷斯滥矣。"

［译文］

孔子在陈国断绝了粮食，跟随的人饿得病倒了，爬不起来。子路不高兴地来见孔子，说："君子也有穷困的时候吗？"孔子说："君子虽穷，仍然坚持着；小人一穷，便什么都干得出来了。"

In Chen provisions ran out. His followers grew too ill to rise. Zilu, with evident vexation, said, "Has even a superior man to be in such want?" The Master said, "A superior man withstands hardship, but the small man, when he is in want, gives way to unbridled license."

［原文］

15·3 子曰："赐也，女以予为多学而识之者与？"对曰："然，非与？"曰："非也，予一以贯之。"

［译文］

孔子说："端木赐！你以为我是广泛地学习而又记得住的

人吗?”子贡回答说:“是的,难道不是这样吗?”孔子说:“不是的,我的学说是用一条忠恕之道贯穿着的。”

The Master said, “Ci, do you think that I am a man who learns much and keeps all of them in memory?” “Yes,” he answered, “Is it not so?” The Master said, “No, I string all into one principle.”

[原文] **15·4** 子曰:“由!知德者鲜矣。”

[译文] 孔子说:“仲由,懂得道德的人很少啊。”

The Master said, “You, those who know virtue are few.”

[原文] **15·5** 子曰:“无为而治者其舜也与?夫何为哉?恭己正南面而已矣。”

[译文] 孔子说:“自己不干什么而能使天下太平的,大概只有舜吧?他干了什么呢?庄严端正地坐在朝廷上罢了。”

The Master said, “To rule doing nothing, that was Shun's way. What did he do? He merely placed himself gravely and reverently in his imperial seat; that was all.”

[原文] **15·6** 子张问行。子曰:“言忠信,行笃敬,虽蛮貊之邦,行矣。言不忠信,行不笃敬,虽州里,行乎哉?立则见其参于前也,在舆则见其倚于衡也,夫然后行。”子张书诸绅。

[译文] 子张问怎样才行得通。孔子说:“说话忠诚老实,行为忠厚严肃,即使在蛮貊国家,也行得通。说话不忠诚讲信用,行为不忠厚严肃,就是在本乡本土,能行得通吗?站立的时候,就仿佛看见‘忠诚老实忠厚严肃’几个字在眼前;在车箱里,也

仿佛看见这几个字刻在车前面的横木上；这样才到处行得通。”子张把这些话写在衣带上。

Zizhang asked how to get on well. The Master said, “Be sincere and true to your every word, and serious and careful in your acts, then you will get on well, even among the rude tribes. If your words are not sincere and truthful, and your acts not serious and careful, will you get on well even in your neighborhood? Standing, see these words ranged before you; driving a carriage, see them written upon the yoke. Then you will get on well.” Zizhang wrote them upon his girdle.

[原文] **15·7** 子曰：“直哉史鱼！邦有道，如矢；邦无道，如矢。君子哉蘧伯玉！邦有道，则仕；邦无道，则可卷而怀之。”

[译文] 孔子说：“史鱼真正直啊！国家政治清明，他像箭一样直，国家政治黑暗，也像箭一样直。蘧伯玉真是位君子啊！国家政治清明，就出来做官，国家政治腐败黑暗，就把本领收藏起来。”

The Master said, “Straight and upright indeed was Shiyu! When the Way prevailed, he was straight like an arrow; when the Way did not prevail, he was straight like an arrow. A superior man indeed was Qu Boyu! When the Way prevailed he took office; when the Way did not prevail, he wrapped his talents up and hid them.”

[原文] **15·8** 子曰：“可与言而不与之言，失人；不可与言而与之言，失言。知者不失人，亦不失言。”

[译文] 孔子说：“可以和他谈话却不谈话，这是错过了人；不可以

和他谈话却去谈话,这是浪费言语。聪明人既不错过人,又不浪费言语。"

The Master said, "Not to speak to one who can be spoken with, is to waste a man. To speak to one who can not be spoken with, is to waste words. The wise never waste a man, nor do they waste their words."

[原文] **15·9** 子曰:"志士仁人,无求生以害仁,有杀身以成仁。"

[译文] 孔子说:"志士仁人,不贪生怕死去损害仁,只有牺牲自己来成全仁。"

The Master said, "The determined scholar and the man of virtue will not seek life at cost of injuring their virtue. They will even sacrifice their lives to fulfil virtue."

[原文] **15·10** 子贡问为仁。子曰:"工欲善其事,必先利其器。居是邦也,事其大夫之贤者,友其士之仁者。"

[译文] 子贡问怎样实行仁德。孔子说:"各种工匠想要搞好工作,一定先修好他的工具。住在这个国家,就要事奉那里大夫中的贤者,结交士人中有仁德的人。"

Zigong asked about the practice of virtue. The Master said, "A workman who wishes to do his work well, must first sharpen his tools. In whatever state you dwell, serve the most worthy among its officers, and make friends with the most virtuous among the scholars."

[原文] **15·11** 颜渊问为邦。子曰:"行夏之时,乘殷之

辂，服周之冕，乐则《韶》《舞》。放郑声，远佞人。郑声淫，佞人殆。”

[译文] 颜渊问怎样治理国家。孔子说：“用夏朝的历法，(它符合季节规律。)乘殷朝的车子，(它简朴。)戴周朝的礼帽，(它华丽。)音乐就用舜的《韶》和武王的《武》。舍弃郑国的乐曲，远离花言巧语谄媚的人。因为郑国乐曲淫荡，花言巧语谄媚的人危险。”

Yan Yuan asked about the governing of a state. The Master said, “Follow the seasons of Xia; drive in a chariot of Yin; wear the ceremonial cap of Zhou; choose for music the Shao and its dance. Banish the tunes of Zhen, and keep far from men of glib tongue. The tunes of Zhen are licentious, men of glib tongue are dangerous.”

[原文] **15·12** 子曰：“人无远虑，必有近忧。”

[译文] 孔子说：“一个人没有长远的考虑，便一定有眼前的忧患。”

The Master said, “If a man takes no thought about what is far off, he will find troubles near at hand.”

[原文] **15·13** 子曰：“已矣乎！吾未见好德如好色者也。”

[译文] 孔子说：“算了吧！我没有见过爱好美德像喜爱美貌一样的人。”

The Master said, “Alas! I have not seen one who loves virtue as he loves beauty!”

[原文] **15·14** 子曰：“臧文仲其窃位者与！知柳下惠之贤而不与立也。”

[译文] 孔子说:“臧文仲大概是个做官而不干事的人吧? 他明知道柳下惠贤能,却不给他职位。”

The Master said, “Did not Zang Wen Zhong steal his post? He knew the virtue and the talents of Liuxia Hui, and yet did not recommend Liuxia Hui for standing with him in court.”

[原文] **15·15** 子曰:“躬自厚而薄责于人,则远怨矣。”

[译文] 孔子说:“多责备自己,而少责备别人,就不致招来怨恨了。”

The Master said, “He who demands much from himself and little from others, will keep himself from resentment.”

[原文] **15·16** 子曰:“不曰‘如之何,如之何’者,吾末如之何也已矣。”

[译文] 孔子说:“一个人不想想怎么办、怎么办的,我也拿他不知道怎么办才好。”

The Master said, “When a man does not continually ask himself ‘what am I to do about this? What am I to do about this?’, I really do not know what I am to do about him!”

[原文] **15·17** 子曰:“群居终日,言不及义,好行小慧,难矣哉!”

[译文] 孔子说:“大家整天在一起,说话没有道理,喜欢卖弄小聪明,这种人很难有出息啊!”

The Master said, “Those who spend a whole day together without any talk of righteousness and are fond of showing off their small smartness are difficult to instruct.”

［原文］ **15·18** 子曰："君子义以为质，礼以行之，孙以出之，信以成之。君子哉！"

［译文］ 孔子说："君子以义为原则，用礼仪去实行，用谦逊的语言来说出它，用诚实的态度完成它，这真是一位君子啊！"

The Master said, "A superior man in everything takes righteousness as his principle. He puts it into practice according to the rules of propriety, speaks it out with modesty and accomplishes it with sincerity. This is indeed a superior man."

［原文］ **15·19** 子曰："君子病无能焉，不病人之不己知也。"

［译文］ 孔子说："君子只担心自己没有能力，不担心别人不知道自己。"

The Master said, "A superior man is distressed by his own want of ability. He is not distressed by others'not knowing him."

［原文］ **15·20** 子曰："君子疾没世而名不称焉。"

［译文］ 孔子说："君子担心死后而名声还不被别人称颂。"

The Master said, "A superior man worrys lest he make no reputation for himself when his life is done."

［原文］ **15·21** 子曰："君子求诸己，小人求诸人。"

［译文］ 孔子说："君子要求自己，小人要求别人。"

The Master said, "A superior man makes demands upon himself; a small man makes demands upon others."

［原文］ **15·22** 子曰："君子矜而不争，群而不党。"

[译文] 孔子说："君子庄矜而不争执，合群而不闹宗派。"

The Master said, "A superior man is dignified, not quarrelsome; sociable, not a partisan."

[原文] **15·23** 子曰："君子不以言举人，不以人废言。"

[译文] 孔子说："君子不因别人话说得好听便提拔他，不因为别人品德不好而废弃正确的话。"

The Master said, "A superior man does not promote a man simply for his words; nor does he reject his good words because of the man."

[原文] **15·24** 子贡问曰："有一言而可以终身行之者乎？"子曰："其恕乎！己所不欲，勿施于人。"

[译文] 子贡问道："有没有一句可以毕生奉行的话呢？"孔子说："大概是'恕'吧！自己所不想要的，不要加在别人身上。"

Zigong asked, "Is there any single saying that one can act upon for all one's life?" The Master said, "Conscientiousness to others (Shu), perhaps. What you do not want done to yourself, do not do to others."

[原文] **15·25** 子曰："吾之于人也，谁毁谁誉？如有所誉者，其有所试矣。斯民也，三代之所以直道而行也。"

[译文] 孔子说："我对于别人，诋毁了谁？称赞了谁？如果我有所称赞，是经过了考验的。夏、商、周三代的人都如此，所以他们都能走正直的道路。"

The Master said, "In my dealings with men, whom do I blame? Whom do I praise? Or if I do praise anybody, it is after trial. Because of these people the three dynasties pursued the path of straightforwardness."

[原文] **15·26** 子曰:"吾犹及史之阙文也。有马者借人乘之,今亡矣夫!"

[译文] 孔子说:"我还能够看到史书中存疑的地方。有马的人,先借给别人使用,今天却没有这种人了。"

The Master said, "I can still see blank spaces in history books. An owner of a horse would lend him to others to ride. Today there are no such things!"

[原文] **15·27** 子曰:"巧言乱德。小不忍,则乱大谋。"

[译文] 孔子说:"花言巧语败坏道德。小事情不能忍耐,就会败坏大事情。"

The Master said, "Clever talk confounds virtue; impatience of trifles confounds great projects."

[原文] **15·28** 子曰:"众恶之,必察焉;众好之,必察焉。"

[译文] 孔子说:"大家都厌恶他,一定要考察一下;大家都喜欢他,一定要考察一下。"

The Master said. "When everyone hates a man, it is necessary to examine into the case; when everyone loves a man, it is necessary to examine into the case."

[原文] **15·29** 子曰:"人能弘道,非道弘人。"

[译文] 孔子说:"人能够把'道'发扬光大,不是'道'能够把人发扬光大。"

The Master said, "A man can enlarge the Way; but there is no Way that can enlarge a man."

[原文] 15·30 子曰:"过而不改,是谓过矣。"

[译文] 孔子说:"错了却不改正,这就叫错误了。"

The Master said, "To have faults and not to correct them, —this, indeed, is to have faults."

[原文] 15·31 子曰:"吾尝终日不食,终夜不寝,以思,无益,不如学也。"

[译文] 孔子说:"我曾经整日不吃,整夜不睡,去冥思苦想,没有什么益处,还不如去学习。"

The Master said, "I once spent in thinking the whole day without food and the whole night without sleep. It was no use. To learn is better."

[原文] 15·32 子曰:"君子谋道不谋食。耕也,馁在其中矣;学也,禄在其中矣。君子忧道不忧贫。"

[译文] 孔子说:"君子谋求学问,不谋求衣食。耕田要饿肚皮;学习可以得到俸禄。君子担忧得不到学问,不担忧贫穷。"

The Master said, "A superior man aims at truth; he does not aim at food. Ploughing may end in famine; learning may end in rank and pay. But a superior man is anxious lest he should not get truth; he is not anxious lest poverty should come upon him."

[原文] 15·33 子曰:"知及之,仁不能守之;虽得之,必失之。知及之,仁能守之。不庄以涖之,则民不敬。知

及之，仁能守之，庄以涖之，动之不以礼，未善也。"

［译文］ 孔子说："靠聪明才智得到了官职，不用仁德保持它，纵然得到了，一定会丧失。靠聪明才智得到了官职，用仁德保持它，如果不庄重严肃地治理百姓，百姓就不会恭恭敬敬。靠聪明才智得到了官职，用仁德保持它，庄重严肃地治理百姓，如果不用礼法去动员百姓，那也是不完善的。"

The Master said, "When a man's wisdom is sufficient to bring him into power, if his virtue is not sufficient to enable him to hold, though he gets it, he will lose again. When his wisdom is sufficient to bring him into power, and he has virtue enough to hold it fast, if he cannot govern with dignity, the people will not respect him. When his wisdom is sufficient to bring him into power, he has virtue enough to hold it fast, and he governs also with dignity, yet if he does not rule the people according to the rules of propriety, full excellence is not reached."

［原文］ **15·34** 子曰："君子不可小知而可大受也，小人不可大受而可小知也。"

［译文］ 孔子说："君子不可以用小事去考验他，却可以承担重大任务；小人不可以承担重大任务，却可以用小事去考验他。"

The Master said, "A superior man cannot be known in small matters, but he may be entrusted with great responsibilities. The small man may not be entrusted with great responsibilities, but he may be known in small matters."

［原文］ **15·35** 子曰："民之于仁也，甚于水火。水火，吾见蹈而死者矣，未见蹈仁而死者也。"

[译文] 孔子说："百姓需要仁德，胜过需要水火。水和火，我看见有人投入到那里面去而死了的，却没见过践行仁德而死了的。"

The Master said, "Virtue is more to the people than fire and water. I have seen men die from treading fire and water, but I have never seen a man die from treading on virtue."

[原文] **15·36** 子曰："当仁，不让于师。"

[译文] 孔子说："面对着仁德的事情，对老师也不谦让。"

The Master said, "When it comes to virtue, one need not avoid competing with one's teacher."

[原文] **15·37** 子曰："君子贞而不谅。"

[译文] 孔子说："君子讲究大信用，不讲究小信用。"

The Master said, "From a superior man consistency is expected, but not blind fidelity."

[原文] **15·38** 子曰："事君，敬其事而后其食。"

[译文] 孔子说："事奉君主，严肃认真地工作，把俸禄的事放在后面。"

The Master said, "In serving his prince, one should be intent upon work, not bent upon the pay."

[原文] **15·39** 子曰："有教无类。"

[译文] 孔子说："人人我都进行教育，没有任何区别。"

The Master said, "There is no distinction of castes in instruction."

[原文] **15·40** 子曰："道不同，不相为谋。"

[译文] 孔子说："主张不同，不互相商量问题。"

The Master said, "Those who follow a different Way cannot take counsel together."

[原文] **15·41** 子曰："辞达而已矣。"

[译文] 孔子说："言辞能够表达意思就行了。"

The Master said, "In speeches all that matters is to convey the meaning."

[原文] **15·42** 师冕见，及阶，子曰："阶也。"及席，子曰："席也。"皆坐，子告之曰："某在斯，某在斯。"

师冕出。子张问曰："与师言之道与？"子曰："然；固相师之道也。"

[译文] 一位叫冕的乐师来进见孔子，走到台阶边，孔子说："这是台阶。"到了坐席前，又说："这是坐席。"都坐定了，（因为乐师冕是瞎子，）孔子告诉他说："我在这里，我在这里。"

师冕出来了。子张问："这是和乐师谈话的方法吗？"孔子说："对，这是帮助乐师的方法。"

The music-master Mian① came to visit Confucius. When they reached the steps, the Master said, "Here are the steps." When they reach the mat, the Master said, "Here is the mat." When all were seated, the Master told him, "So-and-so is here; so-and-so is here."

When the music-master had left, Zizhang said, "Is this the way to speak to a music-master?" The Master said, "Yes. This is surely the Way to help a music-master."

[注释] ① The man being blind, like most musicians in the East.

季氏篇第十六

[原文]

16·1 季氏将伐颛臾。冉有、季路见于孔子曰："季氏将有事于颛臾。"

孔子曰："求！无乃尔是过与？夫颛臾，昔者先王以为东蒙主，且在邦域之中矣，是社稷之臣也。何以伐为？"

冉有曰："夫子欲之，吾二臣者皆不欲也。"

孔子曰："求！周任有言曰：'陈力就列，不能者止。'危而不持，颠而不扶，则将焉用彼相矣？且尔言过矣，虎兕出于柙，龟玉毁于椟中，是谁之过与？"

冉有曰："今夫颛臾，固而近于费。今不取，后世必为子孙忧。"

孔子曰："求！君子疾夫舍曰欲之而必为之辞。丘也闻有国有家者，不患寡而患不均，不患贫而患不安。盖均无贫，和无寡，安无倾。夫如是，故远人不服，则修文德以来之。既来之，则安之。今由与求也，相夫子，远人不服，而不能来也；邦分崩离析，而不能守也；而谋动干戈于邦内。吾恐季孙之忧，不在颛臾，而在萧墙之内也。"

[译文]

季氏准备攻打颛臾。冉有、子路去见孔子，说："季氏准备对颛臾使用武力。"

孔子说："冉求！这难道不应该责备你吗？颛臾，上代君王曾经授权给他主持东蒙山的祭祀，而且那地方早已在鲁国疆域之中，是鲁国的臣属，为什么要去攻打它呢？”

冉有说：“季孙要这么干，我们两个都不同意。”

孔子说：“冉求！周任有句话说：‘献出自己的力量，能够做到的才去就职；不能，就不干。’瞎子遇到危险，助手不去扶持；将要摔倒了，助手也不去搀扶，那又要助手干什么呢？你的话是错了。老虎犀牛从笼子里逃了出来，龟壳、美玉在匣子里毁坏了，这是谁的过错呢？”

冉有说：“颛臾现在城墙很坚固，而且离季氏的封地费邑很近。现在不攻取下来，后世一定会给子孙留下祸害。”

孔子说：“冉求！君子就讨厌不说自己贪得无厌，却一定另找托辞。我听说过：无论诸侯或者大夫，不担心贫穷，而担心财富不平均；不担心人口稀少，而担心境内不安宁。因为财富平均，便无所谓贫穷；境内和睦团结，便不会觉得人口稀少；境内安宁，便不会觉得有倾覆的危险。如果这样，远方的人还不归服，便修明仁义礼教使他们自动归服。他们已经归服了，就得使他们安心。现在仲由和冉求，你们辅助季氏，远方的人不归服，而不能使他们自动来归；国家支离破碎，而不能保全住；反而要在国内动用武力。我担心季孙的忧患不在颛臾，而在自己宫廷里面。”

The Head of Ji family was going to attack Zhuanyu①. Ran You and Jilu②came to see Confucius and said, “The Head of the Ji family is going to use military forces against Zhuanyu.”

Confucius said, “Qiu! is it not you who are in fault? Zhuanyu was long ago appointed by the former king to preside over the sacrifices to the Mount Dongmeng. Moreover, it lies within the boundaries of our state, and it is a vassal state of ours. Why are you going to attack it?”

Ran You said, “Our lord wishes it; neither of us two ministers wishes it."

The Master said, "Qiu, there are the words of Zhou Ren③, 'He who can put forth his ability takes his place in the ranks of office; he who cannot, retires from it.' Of what use is such a guide to a blind man, who sees him tottering, but does not support him, sees him falling, but does not prop him up? Moreover, your plea is a false one. When a tiger or a buffalo escapes from its cage, when a tortoise-shell or jade is broken in its box, whose fault is it?"

Ran You said, "Now Zhuanyu is strongly fortified and is close to Bei④; if it is not taken today, in days to come it will certainly bring trouble to our sons and grandsons."

Confucius said, "Qiu, a superior man hates the man who makes excuses instead of directly saying 'I want it'. I have heard that rulers of states and chiefs of families are not troubled about poverty, but are troubled about misapportionments; that they are not troubled lest their people should be few, but troubled lest they should be unstable. For, if all is well-apportioned, there will be no poverty; if they are in harmony, there will be no lack of men; if stability reigns, there will be no danger of collapse. If all these are done, and yet the people of faroff lands still do not submit, then the ruler should attract them by encouraging ritual and music. Once they have been attracted, they must be made contented and tranquil. Now, here are you, You and Qiu, assisting your lord, the people of far lands do not submit to him, and he cannot attract them to him. In his own state there are divisions and tottery, disruption and cleft, but he cannot save it. And yet he is planning to use military force within the borders of his own land. I am afraid that the troubles of the Ji family will not rise in Zhuanyu, they will rise within his own palace wall."

[注释] ① A small feudatory state within the borders of Lu.

② Zilu. He and Ran You were at the time in the service of the Ji family.

③ A ancient historiographer.

④ The chief castle of the Ji family.

[原文] **16·2** 孔子曰:"天下有道,则礼乐征伐自天子出;天下无道,则礼乐征伐自诸侯出。自诸侯出,盖十世希不失矣;自大夫出,五世希不失矣;陪臣执国命,三世希不失矣。天下有道,则政不在大夫。天下有道,则庶人不议。"

[译文] 孔子说:"天下政治清明,制礼作乐和出兵征讨由天子决定;天下腐败黑暗,制礼作乐和出兵征讨由诸侯决定。由诸侯决定,大概传到十代以后,他们很少有不丧失权柄的;由大夫决定,传到五代以后,很少有不丧失权柄的;若是大夫的家臣把持国家大权,传到三代便很少有不丧失的了。天下政治清明,国家最高政治权力不会由大夫把持。天下政治清明,百姓不会议论纷纷。"

The Master said, "When the Way prevails under Heaven, all orders concerning ceremonies, music and punitive expeditions are issued by the Son of Heaven (emperor). When the Way does not prevail, such orders are issued by the feudal princes. When such orders are issued by the feudal princes, the dynasty will rarely last for ten generations. When they are issued by the state ministers, the dynasty will rarely last for five generations. When the retainers of the great officers sway a state's fate, the dynasty will rarely last for three generations. When the Way prevails under Heaven, power does not lie with ministers. When the Way prevails under Heaven, the common people do not keep on talking about public affairs."

[原文]

16·3 孔子曰:"禄之去公室五世矣,政逮于大夫四世矣,故夫三桓之子孙微矣。"

[译文]

孔子说:"鲁国政权离开鲁君已经有五代了;政权落到卿大夫手中已经有四代了,所以桓公的三房子孙也衰微了。"

Confucius said, "The state power has left the ducal house of Lu for five generations; the government has been in the hands of the great officers for four generations. On this account, the descendants of the Three Huan① are fast declining."

[注释]

① The three families, Meng, Shu, and Ji.

[原文]

16·4 孔子曰:"益者三友,损者三友。友直,友谅,友多闻,益矣。友便辟,友善柔,友便佞,损矣。"

[译文]

孔子说:"有益的朋友有三种,有害的朋友也有三种。和正直的人交朋友,和诚实的人交朋友,和见闻广博的人交朋友,便受益了。和逢迎谄媚的人交朋友,和当面恭维、背后毁谤的人交朋友,和夸夸其谈、华而不实的人交朋友,便有害了。"

Confucius said, "There are three sorts of friends which are advantageous, and three which are harmful. Friendship with the upright; friendship with the sincere; friendship with those who have heard much: —these are advantageous. Friendship with the fawning; friendship with the insinuatingly soft; friendship with the glib-tongued: —these are harmful."

［原文］ **16·5 孔子曰："益者三乐，损者三乐。乐节礼乐，乐道人之善，乐多贤友，益矣。乐骄乐，乐佚游，乐晏乐，损矣。"**

［译文］ 孔子说："有益的乐趣有三种，有害的乐趣也有三种。以得到礼乐的调节为快乐，以宣扬别人的好处为快乐，以交了不少贤明人物为快乐，这就受益了。以骄奢淫逸为快乐，以游荡忘返为快乐，以聚众大吃大喝为快乐，便有害了。"

Confucius said, "There are three sorts of pleasures which are advantageous, and three which are harmful. The pleasure in being adjusted by ritual and music; the pleasure in speaking of the good of others; and the pleasure in having worthy friends: —these pleasures are advantageous. The pleasure in profligate enjoyments; the pleasure in idle gadding about; the pleasure in the joys of feasting: —these pleasures are harmful."

［原文］ **16·6 孔子曰："侍于君子有三愆：言未及之而言谓之躁，言及之而不言谓之隐，未见颜色而言谓之瞽。"**

［译文］ 孔子说："陪侍君子容易犯三种过失：不该他说话时却急于先说，叫做急躁；该他说时却不开口叫做隐瞒；不看别人的脸色便贸然开口，叫做瞎了眼睛。"

Confucius said, "There are three mistakes that are liable to be made when waiting upon a superior man. To speak before the time has come, this is called rashness. Not to speak when the time has come, this is called concealment. To speak without first looking at the countenance of the superior man, this is called blindness."

[原文]

16·7 孔子曰:“君子有三戒:少之时,血气未定,戒之在色;及其壮也,血气方刚,戒之在斗;及其老也,血气既衰,戒之在得。”

[译文]

孔子说:“君子有三件应该警惕戒备的事:年轻的时候,血气还没有稳定,警戒自己不要迷恋女色;到了壮年,血气正旺盛,警戒自己不要逞强相斗;等到老了,血气已经衰弱,警戒自己不要贪得无厌。”

Confucius said, “There are three things which the superior man guards against. In youth, when the physical powers are not yet settled, he guards against lust. In his prime of life, when the physical powers are full of vigour, he guards against strife. In old age, when the physical powers are decaying, he guards against greed.”

[原文]

16·8 子曰:“君子有三畏:畏天命,畏大人,畏圣人之言。小人不知天命而不畏也,狎大人,侮圣人之言。”

[译文]

孔子说:“君子惧怕三件事:惧怕天命,惧怕权贵人物,惧怕圣人的言论。小人不懂得天命,因而不惧怕,亵渎权贵人物,侮慢圣人的言论。”

Confucius said, “There are three things of which a superior man is in awe. He is in awe of the will of Heaven. He is in awe of great men. He is in awe of the words of sages. The small man does not know the will of Heaven and so he does not stand in awe of it. He is disrespectful to great men. He scoffs at the words of sages.”

［原文］ **16·9** 孔子曰："生而知之者上也，学而知之者次也；困而学之，又其次也；困而不学，民斯为下矣。"

［译文］ 孔子说："生下来就知道的人是上等；学了才知道的人是次等；遇到困难不得不学的人又次一等；遇到困难而不学习，这种人是最下等的了。"

Confucius said, "Highest are those who are born with innate knowledge. Next are those who get possession of knowledge by learning. After them come those who start learning only when they feel puzzled. As to those who do not learn even when they feel puzzled, they are the lowest of the people."

［原文］ **16·10** 孔子曰："君子有九思：视思明，听思聪，色思温，貌思恭，言思忠，事思敬，疑思问，忿思难，见得思义。"

［译文］ 孔子说："君子有九种事情需要考虑：看要考虑看明白了吗；听要考虑听清楚了吗；脸色要考虑温和吗；容貌要考虑恭敬吗；言语要考虑忠实吗；工作要考虑认真吗；疑惑要考虑怎样去提问；愤怒要考虑会不会有后患；遇见有所得，要考虑是否该得。"

Confucius said, "A superior man has nine cares. In seeing he is careful to see clearly; in hearing he is careful to hear distinctly; in his countenance he is careful to be benign; in his manner to be respectful; in his words to be sincere; in his work to be diligent. When in doubt he is careful to ask others; when he is angry he has a care for the consequences, and when he sees gain to be got, he thinks of righteousness."

［原文］ **16·11** 孔子曰："见善如不及，见不善如探汤。吾见其人矣，吾闻其语矣。隐居以求其志，行义以达其道。吾闻其语矣，未见其人也。"

［译文］ 孔子说："看见善良的，努力追求，好像唯恐赶不上似的；看见邪恶，尽力避开，好像手将伸进沸水里。我遇见过这样的人，也听到过这样的话。避世隐居来保全自己的志向，做合乎正义的事来贯彻自己的主张。我听过这样的话，却没有遇见过这样的人。"

Confucius said, "When seeing good, they pursue it, as if they could not reach it; when seeing evil, they shrink from it, as they would from putting the hand into boiling water: —I have seen such men. I have heard such words. By dwelling in seclusion they seek the fulfilment of their aims; by practising righteousness they carry out their principles: —I have heard these words, but I have not seen such men."

［原文］ **16·12** 齐景公有马千驷，死之日，民无德而称焉。伯夷、叔齐饿于首阳之下，民到于今称之。其斯之谓与？

［译文］ 齐景公有马四千匹，到他死的时候，百姓都认为他没有什么德行值得称赞的。伯夷、叔齐饿死在首阳山下，百姓到今天还称赞他们。大概说的就是这个意思吧？

Duke Jing of Qi had a thousand teams of horses, but on the day of his death, the people could think of no single virtue for which to praise him. Boyi and Shuqi died of hunger at the foot of Shouyang Mountain, yet the people praise them down to this very day. Is not the saying illustrated by this?[1]

[注释]

① Some words lacked here, or this sentence was out of place.

[原文]

16·13 陈亢问于伯鱼曰:“子亦有异闻乎?”

对曰:“未也。尝独立,鲤趋而过庭。曰:‘学《诗》乎?’对曰:‘未也。’‘不学《诗》,无以言。’鲤退而学《诗》。他日,又独立,鲤趋而过庭。曰:“学礼乎?’对曰:‘未也。’‘不学礼,无以立。’鲤退而学礼。闻斯二者。”

陈亢退而喜曰:“问一得三,闻《诗》,闻礼,又闻君子之远其子也。”

[译文]

陈亢向(孔子的儿子)伯鱼问道:“您在老师那里得到不同于一般人的教授吗?”

伯鱼回答说:“没有。他曾经独自站着,我快步走过庭中。他说:‘学过《诗》吗?’我回答说:‘没有。’他说:‘不学《诗》,就不善于说话。’我退回来就学《诗》。另一天,他又独自站着,我又快步地走过庭中。他说:‘学了礼吗?’我回答说:‘没有。’他说:‘不学礼,便在社会上无法站稳脚跟。’我回来便去学礼。我只听到这两件事。”

陈亢回去高兴地说:“问一件事,知道了三件事。听到学《诗》,听到学礼,还听到君子不偏爱自己的儿子。”

Chen Kang[1] asked Boyu[2], “Have you heard any lessons different from what we have heard?”

Boyu replied, “No. Once when he was standing alone and I was hurrying past him across the court-yard, he said to me, ‘Have you learned poems?’ I answered, ‘No.’ ‘If you don’t study poems, you will have no holds on words.’ So I retired and learned the poems. Another day he was standing alone, and as I hurried across the court-yard, he said to me, 'Have you studied the rules of propriety?' I answered, 'No.' 'If you don't study the rules of propriety,' he said, 'you can't take your stand.' I then retired and studied the rules of propriety. These two things I have heard from him."

Chen kang went away delighted, saying, "I asked one thing, but got three things. I have heard about poems. I have heard about the rules of propriety. I have also heard that the superior man keeps his son at a distance."

[注释] ① i. e. zi Qin.

② Kong Li, Confucius's son.

[原文] **16·14** 邦君之妻，君称之曰夫人，夫人自称曰小童；邦人称之曰君夫人，称诸异邦曰寡小君，异邦人称之亦曰君夫人。

[译文] 国君的妻子，国君称她为夫人，她称自己为小童；本国人称她为君夫人，对外国人便称她为寡小君，外国人也称她为君夫人。

The wife of the prince of a state is called by him Fu Ren. She calls herself Xiao Tong. The people of the state call her Jun Fu Ren, and to the people of other states, they call her Gua Xiao Jun. The people of other states also call her Jun Fu Ren.

阳货篇第十七

［原文］

17·1 阳货欲见孔子,孔子不见,归孔子豚。

孔子时其亡也,而往拜之。

遇诸涂。

谓孔子曰:“来!予与尔言。”曰:“怀其宝而迷其邦,可谓仁乎?”曰:“不可。好从事而亟失时,可谓知乎?”曰:“不可。日月逝矣,岁不我与。”

孔子曰:“诺,吾将仕矣。”

［译文］

阳货想要孔子去见他,孔子不去见,阳货送孔子(一头蒸熟了的)小猪。

孔子探听到他外出时去拜谢他。

在路上碰到了。

阳货对孔子说:“来!我和你说话。”阳货说:“怀有一身本领,却听任国家一塌糊涂,可以叫做仁吗?”他自己接着说:“不可以。”“一个人喜欢做事情,却屡屡错过机会,可以叫做聪明吗?”他接着说:“不可以。时光一天天过去了,岁月不会等待我们。”

孔子这才说:“好吧,我准备做官了。”

Yang Huo① wanted Confucius to see him, but Confucius would not see him. He sent Confucius a sucking pig.

Confucius chose a time when he knew Yang Huo was not at home, and went to thank him.

Confucius met him, however, on the road.

He said to Confucius, “Come, I have something to say to

you." He then said, "Can he be called benevolent, who keeps his talents in his bosom, and leaves his country to confusion?" He replied by himself, "Certainly not. Can he be called wise, who longs to be engaged in public employment, and yet time after time misses the opportunity to do so?" He went on saying, "Certainly not. The days and months are gliding by, the years do not wait for us."

Confucius said, "All right, I will go into office."

[注释] ① The all-powerful, unscrupulous retainer of Ji family.

[原文] **17·2** 子曰:"性相近也,习相远也。"

[译文] 孔子说:"人的本性本来互相接近,因为受不同环境习俗的熏陶便大不一样。"

The Master said, "By nature, men are nearly alike; by practice, they get to be far apart."

[原文] **17·3** 子曰:"唯上知与下愚不移。"

[译文] 孔子说:"只有头等聪明人和极端愚蠢的人,才是改变不了的。"

The Master said, "It is only the very wisest and the very stupidest who cannot change."

[原文] **17·4** 子之武城,闻弦歌之声。夫子莞尔而笑,曰:"割鸡焉用牛刀?"

子游对曰:"昔者偃也闻诸夫子曰:'君子学道则爱人,小人学道则易使也。'"

子曰:"二三子!偃之言是也。前言戏之耳。"

[译文] 孔子到武城去,听到弹琴唱歌的声音。孔子微笑着说:"杀鸡,哪里用得着宰牛刀呢?(治理这小地方,用得着如此礼乐教化吗?)"

子游回答说:"以前我听见老师说过:'君子学习了道理便有仁爱之心,小人学习了道理便容易听使唤。'"

孔子说:"你们听着,言偃的话是对的。我刚才的话不过是跟他开玩笑罢了。"

When the Master came to Wucheng①, he heard the sound of stringed instruments and singing. With a gentle smile, he said, "Why use an ox-knife to kill a chicken?"

Ziyou replied, "Master, I remember once hearing you say that the man of high station who has studied the Way will love mankind; the common people who have studied the Way are easy to rule."

The Master said, "My disciples, Yan's② words are right. What I said just now was only meant as a joke."

[注释] ① Where Ziyou was in command.

② Ziyou's personal name.

[原文] **17·5 公山弗扰以费畔,召,子欲往。**

子路不说,曰:"末之也,已,何必公山氏之之也?"

子曰:"夫召我者,而岂徒哉?如有用我者,吾其为东周乎?"

[译文] 公山弗扰盘踞着费邑图谋造反,叫孔子去,孔子打算去。

子路不高兴,说:"没地方去便算了,为什么一定要去公山氏那里呢?"

孔子说:"那个叫我去的人,难道是白白叫我去吗?如果有人用我,我将使周文王、武王的德政在东方再度兴起啊!"

Gongshan Furao①, when he held Bei in rebellion, he sent for the Master, who was inclined to go.

Zilu was displeased, and said, "If you have no place to go, that is all right. Why must you go to see Gongshan?"

The Master said, "He has sent for me, can it be for nothing? If anyone were to use me, I believe I could make a 'Zhou in the east'."

[注释] ① Warden of Bei, the chief stronghold of the Ji family.

[原文] **17·6 子张问仁于孔子。孔子曰:"能行五者于天下为仁矣。"**

"请问之。"曰:"恭,宽,信,敏,惠。恭则不侮,宽则得众,信则人任焉,敏则有功,惠则足以使人。"

[译文] 子张问孔子怎样实行仁政。孔子说:"能够在普天之下实行五种品德的,便是仁德了。"

子张说:"请教哪五种?"孔子说:"庄重,宽厚,诚实,勤敏,慈惠。庄重就不会遭受侮辱,宽厚就会得到大众的拥护,诚实就会得到别人的任用,勤敏工作就有成绩,慈惠就能很好地使唤别人。"

Zizhang asked Confucius about perfect virtue. Confucius said, "He who could put five things into practice everywhere under Heaven would be a man of perfect virtue."

Zizhang said, "May I ask what they are?" Confucius said, "Gravity, open-heartedness, sincerity, earnestness and kindness. Gravity escapes insult; open-heartedness wins all; sincerity gains men's trust; earnestness brings success; kindness gets service from the people."

[原文]

17·7 佛肸召,子欲往。

子路曰:"昔者由也闻诸夫子曰:'亲于其身为不善者,君子不入也。'佛肸以中牟畔,子之往也,如之何?"

子曰:"然,有是言也。不曰坚乎,磨而不磷;不曰白乎,涅而不缁。吾岂匏瓜也哉?焉能系而不食?"

[译文]

佛肸叫孔子去,孔子打算去。

子路说:"从前我听见老师说过:'亲自做坏事的人那里,君子是不去的。'如今佛肸盘踞中牟叛乱,您要去,怎么说得过去呢?"

孔子说:"对,我有过这话。不是说坚固的东西,磨也磨不薄吗?不是说白的东西,染也染不黑吗?我难道是匏瓜吗?哪能够只被人悬挂着而不给人食用呢?"

Bi Xi① summoned the Master, and he was inclined to go.

Zilu said, "Master, I have heard you say, 'When a man is in his own person doing what is evil, a superior man will not enter his house.' Bi Xi is holding Zhongmu in revolt. If you go to him, what shall be said?"

The Master said, "Yes, I did say so. But is it not said that, if a thing is really hard, no grinding can make it thin? Is it not said that, if a thing is really white, no steeping can make it black? Am I a bitter gourd? How can I be only fit to hang up but not to eat?"

[注释]

① A Jin officer.

[原文]

17·8 子曰:"由也!女闻六言六蔽矣乎?"对曰:"未也。"

"居！吾语女。好仁不好学，其蔽也愚；好知不好学，其蔽也荡；好信不好学，其蔽也贼；好直不好学，其蔽也绞；好勇不好学，其蔽也乱；好刚不好学，其蔽也狂。"

[译文] 孔子说："仲由呀！你听说过六种品德会带来六种弊病吗？"子路回答说："没有。"

孔子说："坐下！我告诉你。爱好仁德，却不喜好学问，它的弊病是容易被愚弄；爱耍聪明却不喜好学问，它的弊病是放荡不羁；喜好诚实却不喜好学问，它的弊病是（容易被人利用）害了自己；喜爱直率却不喜好学问，它的弊病是说话尖刻伤人；喜爱勇敢却不喜好学问，它的弊病是捣乱闯祸；喜爱刚强却不喜好学问，它的弊病是胆大妄为。"

The Master said, "ZhongYou, have you heard the six virtues to which six degenerations are attached?" You replied, "No."

The Master said, "Sit down and I will tell you. Love of human-heartedness without love of learning degenerates into silliness. Love of wisdom without love of learning degenerates into presumption. Love of honesty without love of learning degenerates into being easily used and harming oneself. Love of straightforwardness without love of learning degenerates into harshness. Love of courage without love of learning degenerates into turbulance. Love of firmness without love of learning degenerates into arrogance."

[原文] **17·9** 子曰："小子何莫学夫《诗》？《诗》，可以兴，可以观，可以群，可以怨。迩之事父，远之事君；多识于鸟兽草木之名。"

[译文] 孔子说："学生们为什么不学习《诗》呢？学《诗》可以培养联想力，可以提高观察力，可以锻炼合群性，可以学得讽刺方法。近可以运用其中的道理事奉父母，远可以用来服事君主，而且可以多多认识一些鸟兽草木的名称。"

The Master said, "My disciples, why do you not study the Book of Poetry? The Odes will help you to stimulate the mind, to deepen the observantion. They can teach you the art of sociability and make you know how to demonstrate with your superiors. They may be used at home in the service of your parents; abroad, in the service of the prince. Moreover, they will widen your acquaintance with the names of birds, beasts, plants and trees."

[原文] **17·10** 子谓伯鱼曰："女为《周南》、《召南》矣乎？人而不为《周南》、《召南》，其犹正墙面而立也与？"

[译文] 孔子对伯鱼说："你研究过《诗》中《周南》、《召南》吗？一个人不研究《周南》、《召南》，那不好比把脸面对着墙壁站立着吗？（一步也不能前进。）"

The Master said to Boyu, "Have you studied Zhou Nan and Shao Nan[1] yet? The man who has not studied Zhou Nan and Shao Nan is as though he stands with his face right against a wall!"

[注释] ① The first two books of the Book of Poetry.

[原文] **17·11** 子曰："礼云礼云，玉帛云乎哉？乐云乐云，钟鼓云乎哉？"

[译文] 孔子说："礼呀礼呀，仅仅是指玉帛等礼物说的吗？乐呀乐呀，仅仅是指钟鼓等乐器说的吗？"

The Master said, "Ritual, ritual! Are jade and silk all that is meant by ritual? Music, music! Are bells and drums all that is meant by music?"

[原文] **17·12** 子曰："色厉而内荏，譬诸小人，其犹穿窬之盗也与？"

[译文] 孔子说："外表声色严厉，而内心怯弱，若用坏人作比喻，大概像个挖洞跳墙的小偷吧？"

The Master said, "He who assumed an outward air of fierceness while inwardly weak, in comparison with the small man, is like a thief who crawls through a hole in the wall."

[原文] **17·13** 子曰："乡愿，德之贼也。"

[译文] 孔子说："好好先生，是败坏道德的人。"

The Master said, "The good careful people of the villages spoil the true virtue."

[原文] **17·14** 子曰："道听而途说，德之弃也。"

[译文] 孔子说："在路上听到传言就四处传播，这是对道德的背弃。"

The Master said, "To spread what you have heard on the way, is to abandon virtue."

[原文] **17·15** 子曰："鄙夫可与事君也与哉？其未得之也，患得之。既得之，患失之。苟患失之，无所不至矣。"

[译文] 孔子说："鄙陋之人，难道可以和他一道事奉君主吗？当他没有得到职位的时候，就怕得不到；已经得到了，又怕失去

它。如果怕失去,就无所不用其极了。"

The Master said, "How can one serve the prince along with those mean creatures? While they have not got office, their anxiety is how to get it. When they have got it, their anxiety is how to avoid losing it. When they are anxious for losing it, there is no length to which they will not go."

[原文] **17·16 子曰:"古者民有三疾,今也或是之亡也。古之狂也肆,今之狂也荡;古之矜也廉,今之矜也忿戾;古之愚也直,今之愚也诈而已矣。"**

[译文] 孔子说:"古代有三种毛病,今天连这都没有了。古代的狂人肆意直言,如今的狂人便放荡不羁了;古代矜持自尊的人威不可犯,现在矜持自尊的人一味恼怒蛮横;古代愚笨的人还直率,现在愚笨的人只是欺诈罢了。"

The Master said, "In old days, men had three failings, which have, perhaps, died out today. The impetuous of old days were impatient of small restraints; the impetuous today are utterly insubordinate. The stern dignity of old days were stiff and gravely reserved; the stern dignity today are touchy and quarrelsome. The simple men of old days were straightforward; the simple men today show themselves in sheer deceit."

[原文] **17·17 子曰:"巧言令色,鲜矣仁。"**

[译文] 孔子说:"花言巧语,一副讨好的脸色,这种人,没有多少仁德。"

The Master said, "Honey words and flattering looks seldom speak of virtue."

[原文] **17·18** 子曰:“恶紫之夺朱也,恶郑声之乱雅乐也,恶利口之覆邦家者。”

[译文] 孔子说:“我厌恶紫色夺去了大红色的光彩,厌恶郑国的乐曲扰乱了典雅的乐曲,厌恶尖嘴利舌倾覆国家的人。”

The Master said, “I hate to see purple taking away the lustre of red. I hate to see the songs of Zheng corrupting the count music. I hate those who with their sharp mouths overthrow kingdoms.”

[原文] **17·19** 子曰:“予欲无言。”子贡曰:“子如不言,则小子何述焉?”子曰:“天何言哉? 四时行焉,百物生焉,天何言哉?”

[译文] 孔子说:“我想不说什么了。”子贡说:“您如果不说,那我们传述什么呢?”孔子说:“天说了什么呢? 四季照样运行,百物照样生长,天说了什么呢?”

The Master said, “I'd like not to speak.” Zigong said, “If you, Master, do not speak, what shall we, your disciples, have to record?” The Master said, “Does Heaven speak? The four seasons run their courses, and all things are continually being produced. Does Heaven speak?”

[原文] **17·20** 孺悲欲见孔子,孔子辞以疾。将命者出户,取瑟而歌,使之闻之。

[译文] 孺悲想要见孔子,孔子托词有病不见。传达的人刚出房门,孔子拿起瑟边弹边唱,故意使孺悲听到。

Ru Bei① wanted to see Confucius. Confucius excused himself on the plea of sickness. But when the messenger was going out through the door, Confucius took up his Se and sang to it, in order that the messenger might hear him.

[注释] ① A person of Lu.

[原文] **17·21** 宰我问："三年之丧，期已久矣。君子三年不为礼，礼必坏；三年不为乐，乐必崩。旧谷既没，新谷既升，钻燧改火，期可已矣。"

子曰："食夫稻，衣夫锦，于女安乎？"

曰："安。"

"女安，则为之！夫君子之居丧，食旨不甘，闻乐不乐，居处不安，故不为也。今女安，则为之！"

宰我出。子曰："予之不仁也！子生三年，然后免于父母之怀。夫三年之丧，天下之通丧也，予也有三年之爱于其父母乎！"

[译文] 宰我问："父母死亡，守孝三年，时间太久了。君子三年不去实行礼仪，礼仪一定会被破坏；三年不去奏音乐，乐曲一定会荒废。旧谷已经吃完了，新谷又已登场，取火的木头轮换了一遍，丧期一年也就可以了。"

孔子说："父母死了不到三年便吃稻米饭，穿锦缎衣，你心里安不安呢？"

宰我说："安。"

孔子说："你心安，你就去干吧！君子在服丧期间，吃美食不觉得味道好，听到好的乐曲不觉得快乐，居住坐立都不安，所以才不那样做。现在你心安，你就去做吧！"

宰我出来后，孔子说："宰予真不仁啊！儿子生下三年，然后才脱离父母怀抱。服丧三年，是天下通行的丧礼，宰予从父母那里难道没有得到三年怀抱的爱抚吗？"

Zai Wo said, "Three years'mourning is too long. If a superior man suspends their practice of propriety for three years, the propriety will decay. If he makes no music for three years, music will certainly be ruined. Within a year, the old grain has already vanished, the new grain has sprung up; and the round of woods for the fire-drill is ended. Surely a year would be enough."

The Master asked, "Would you then feel at ease in eating good rice and wearing silk brocades?"

Zai Wo said, "Quite at ease."

The Master said, "If you can feel at ease, do it. But a superior man, when in mourning, does not enjoy pleasant food, nor does he derive pleasure from music. If he is comfortably lodged in his home, he does not feel at ease either. That is why he abstains from these things. But now you feel at ease, you may do it."

Zai Wo then went out, and the Master said, "A man without human-heartedness! Only when a child is three years old does he leave his parents'arms. The three years'mourning is the universal mourning under heaven. And Yu, did he not enjoy his parents'affection for three years?"

[原文] **17·22 子曰："饱食终日，无所用心，难矣哉！不有博弈者乎？为之，犹贤乎已。"**

[译文] 孔子说："整天吃饱饭，不用一点心思，难得有出息啊！不是有掷采、下棋的游戏吗？干干也比闲散着好。"

The Master said, "Bad it is when a man crams himself with food all day and has nothing to task the mind! Are there not games such as draughts? Playing them would still be better than doing nothing at all."

[原文] **17·23** 子路曰:"君子尚勇乎?"子曰:"君子义以为上,君子有勇而无义为乱,小人有勇而无义为盗。"

[译文] 子路问道:"君子崇尚勇敢吗?"孔子说:"君子认为正义是头等要紧的。君子只讲勇敢不讲正义就会造反作乱,小人只讲勇敢不讲正义就会做强盗。"

Zilu asked, "Does a superior man esteem courage?" The Master said, "A superior man gives the first place to righteousness. If a superior man has courage but no righteousness, he will become turbulent. If a small man has courage but no righteousness, he will become a thief."

[原文] **17·24** 子贡曰:"君子亦有恶乎?"子曰:"有恶:恶称人之恶者,恶居下流而讪上者,恶勇而无礼者,恶果敢而窒者。"

曰:"赐也亦有恶乎?""恶徼以为知者,恶不孙以为勇者,恶讦以为直者。"

[译文] 子贡说:"君子也有憎恶的事吗?"孔子说:"有憎恶的事:憎恶专说别人坏处的人,憎恶在下位而毁谤在上位的人,憎恶勇敢却没有礼貌的人,憎恶勇敢果断却顽固不化的人。"

又说:"端木赐!你也有憎恶的事吗?"子贡说:"我憎恶偷取别人的成果却自以为聪明的人,憎恶毫不谦虚却自以为勇敢的人,憎恶攻击别人的短处却自以为正直的人。"

Zigong said, "Does a superior man has his hatreds also?" The Master said, "He has his hatreds. He hates those who spread evil of others. He hates those who being in a low station slander their superiors. He hates those who have only courage but do not know the rules of propriety. He hates those who are forward and determined but stubborn."

He then asked, "Ci, do you also have hatreds?" Zigong answered, "I hate those who mistake spying for wisdom. I hate those who mistake want of modesty for courage. I hate those who mistake tale-bearing for honesty."

[原文] **17·25** 子曰:"唯女子与小人为难养也,近之则不孙,远之则怨。"

[译文] 孔子说:"只有女子和小人难得和他们共处。亲近了就会无礼,疏远了就会怨恨。"

The Master said, "Only women and small men are very hard to deal with. If you are close to them, they become unruly. If you keep them at a distance, they are discontented."

[原文] **17·26** 子曰:"年四十而见恶焉,其终也已。"

[译文] 孔子说:"到了四十岁还被人讨厌,他这一生也就完了。"

The Master said, "When a man of forty is still disliked, it will be so till the end."

微子篇第十八

［原文］ **18·1** 微子去之，箕子为之奴，比干谏而死。孔子曰："殷有三仁焉。"

［译文］ （殷纣王昏乱残暴，胞兄）微子离开他，（叔叔）箕子做了奴隶，（叔叔）比干劝阻他被处死。孔子说："殷朝有三位仁人。"

Wei Zi① fled from him(tyrant King Zhou). QiZi② became a slave to him. Bigan③ remonstrated with him and was killed. Confucius said, "The Yin dynasty possessed these three men of virtue."

［注释］

① King Zhou's step-brother.

② King Zhou's uncle.

③ King Zhou's uncle.

［原文］ **18·2** 柳下惠为士师，三黜。人曰："子未可以去乎？"曰："直道而事人，焉往而不三黜？枉道而事人，何必去父母之邦？"

［译文］ 柳下惠担任法官，多次被撤职。有人对他说："您不可以离开这里吗？"他说："正直地事奉君主，到哪里去而不多次被撤职呢？不正直地事奉君主，为什么一定要离开祖国呢？"

When Liuxia Hui was chief criminal judge, he was three times dismissed. Someone said to him, "Why not leave the state?" He answered, "If I serve men in an upright way, where can I go and not be three times dismissed? If I choose to serve men in a crooked way, what necessity is there for me to leave my native state?"

［原文］ **18·3** 齐景公待孔子曰："若季氏，则吾不能；以季、孟之间待之。"曰："吾老矣，不能用也。"孔子行。

［译文］ 齐景公讲到怎样对待孔子，说："像鲁君对待季氏那样，我就办不到。我打算用次于季氏、高于孟氏的待遇来对待他。"后来又说："我老了，没有什么作为了。"孔子便离开了齐国。

Duke Jing of Qi, speaking of how to treat Confucius, said, "I cannot treat him as the King of Lu did the head of the Ji family. I will treat him as though he ranked between the head of Ji and the Meng." He also said, "I am old, I cannot accomplish anything more." Confucius then left the state of Qi.

［原文］ **18·4** 齐人归女乐，季桓子受之，三日不朝，孔子行。

［译文］ 齐国送来歌姬舞女，季桓子接受了，一连三天不上朝听政，孔子离去了。

The people of Qi sent to Lu a present of geisha girls. Ji Huan Zi① accepted them, for three days no court was held. Confucius then left Lu.

［注释］ ① Ji Kong Zi's father, a high official of Lu.

［原文］ **18·5** 楚狂接舆歌而过孔子曰："凤兮凤兮！何德之衰？往者不可谏，来者犹可追。已而，已而！今之从政者殆而！"

孔子下，欲与之言。趋而辟之，不得与之言。

[译文] 楚国狂人接舆唱着歌经过孔子车前,唱道:"凤凰呀,凤凰呀!为什么德行这么衰微?过去的已不能挽回,今后的还来得及改正。算了吧,算了吧!今天当政的人物太危险!"

孔子下车,想和他交谈,他赶快避开,孔子没法和他交谈。

Jie Yu,① the madman of Chu, passed by Confucius, singing and saying, "Oh phoenix, phoenix! How dwindled is your virtue! As to the past, reproof is useless; but the future may be remedied. Desist, desist! Peril awaits those who now engage in government."

Confucius got down from his carriage and wanted to speak with him, but Jie Yu hastened away, so that Confucius could not talk with him.

[注释] ① A hermit.

[原文] **18·6** 长沮、桀溺耦而耕,孔子过之,使子路问津焉。

长沮曰:"夫执舆者为谁?"

子路曰:"为孔丘。"

曰:"是鲁孔丘与?"

曰:"是也。"

曰:"是知津矣。"

问于桀溺。

桀溺曰:"子为谁?"

曰:"为仲由。"

曰:"是鲁孔丘之徒与?"

对曰:"然。"

曰:"滔滔者天下皆是也,而谁以易之?且而与其从辟人之士也，岂若从辟世之士哉？”耰而不辍。

子路行以告。

夫子怃然曰：“鸟兽不可与同群，吾非斯人之徒与而谁与？天下有道，丘不与易也。”

［译文］ 长沮、桀溺两人一起耕作，孔子经过那里，叫子路下去询问渡口在哪里。

长沮说：“那驾车子的是谁？”

子路说：“是孔丘。”

他说：“是鲁国的孔丘吗？”

子路说：“是的。”

他便说：“他知道渡口在哪里。”

子路又去问桀溺。

桀溺说：“您是谁？”

子路说：“我是仲由。”

他说：“您是鲁国孔丘的门徒吗？”

子路回答说：“是的。”

他便说：“到处都是像洪水一样恶浊的东西，你们能同谁去改变它呢？而且你与其跟着孔丘那种逃避坏人的人，为什么不跟随我们这些逃避现实的人呢？”一边说，一边不停地覆盖种子。

子路回来报告孔子。

孔子失望地说：“我们不能和鸟兽相处，不同人群中的你们在一起，又同谁在一起呢？天下政治清明，我就不参与改革了。”

Changju and Jieni① were working together in the fields. Confucius happened to pass by them, and sent Zilu to enquire of the ford.

Changju asked, “who is he that holds the reins in the carriage?"

Zilu answered, "It is Kong Qiu."

"Is it Kong Qiu of Lu?" asked he.

"Yes," said Zilu.

Changju said, "He knows the ford."

Zilu then enquired of Jieni.

Jieni asked, "who are you, sir?"

He answered, "I am Zongyou."

"Are you the disciple of Kong Qiu of Lu?" asked Jieni.

"I am." Zilu replied.

Jieni then said to him, "Disorder, like a swelling flood, spreads everywrere, and with whom will you change it? Than follow one who merely flees from bad men, had you not better follow us who flee from the world?" With this he went on covering the seed.

Zilu went back and told the Master, who said disappointedly, "We cannot herd with birds and beasts. If I do not associate with these people, with mankind, with whom shall I associate? If the Way prevailed under Heaven, I should not be trying to chang."

［注释］ ① Two hermits.

［原文］ **18·7** 子路从而后，遇丈人，以杖荷蓧。

子路问曰："子见夫子乎？"

丈人曰："四体不勤，五谷不分。孰为夫子？"植其杖而芸。

子路拱而立。

止子路宿，杀鸡为黍而食之，见其二子焉。

明日，子路行以告。

子曰："隐者也。"使子路反见之。至，则行矣。

子路曰："不仕无义。长幼之节，不可废也；君臣之义，如之何其废之？欲洁其身，而乱大伦。君子之仕也，行其义也。道之不行，已知之矣。"

［译文］ 子路跟随着孔子，走在后面，遇见一个老人，用手杖挑着除草用的工具。

子路问道："您看见我的老师了吗？"

老人说："四肢不劳动，五谷不能分辨，谁是你的老师呢？"老人把手杖插进泥土中就锄草去了。

子路拱着手恭敬地站立着。

老人留子路住宿，杀了鸡，做好黄米饭给子路吃，叫他两个儿子出来相见。

第二天，子路赶上孔子，报告了这件事。

孔子说："这是位隐士。"叫子路回去见他。等子路到原来的地方，他已经搬走了。

子路说："不出来做官是不合情理的。长幼间的礼节不可废弃，君臣间的礼节又怎么可以废弃呢？想使自己清白，却搞乱了君臣间的伦理关系。君子出来做官，为的是履行君臣之义。我们的主张行不通，早已知道了。"

Once when Zilu was following the Master, fell behind and met an old man carrying a tool for weeding(across his shoulder) on a walking stick.

Zilu asked him, "Have you seen my master?"

The old man replied, "You do not toil with your four limbs, nor can you distinguish five kinds of grain; who is your master?"

With this, he planted his walking stick in the ground and began weeding.

Zilu stood by with his hands pressed together.

The old man kept Zilu for the night. He killed a fowl, prepared millet, and feasted him. He also introduced Zilu to his two sons.

Next day Zilu went on his way and reported what had happened to the Master.

The Master said, "He is a recluse." and sent Zilu back to see him. But when he got to the place, he found the old man had gone.

Zilu said, "Not to take office is not right. The relations between old and young may not be set aside, how can the duty that binds minister to prince be set aside? Wishing to maintain his personal purity, he flouts the great relationship. The reason why the superior man tries to go into politics, is because he holds this to be right, even though he is well aware that his principle cannot prevail."

[原文] **18·8** 逸民:伯夷、叔齐、虞仲、夷逸、朱张、柳下惠、少连。子曰:"不降其志,不辱其身,伯夷、叔齐与!"谓"柳下惠、少连,降志辱身矣,言中伦,行中虑,其斯而已矣。"谓"虞仲、夷逸,隐居放言,身中清,废中权。我则异于是,无可无不可。"

[译文] 被遗落的人才有伯夷、叔齐、虞仲、夷逸、朱张、柳下惠、少连。孔子说:"不降低自己的志气,不辱没自己的身份,要算伯夷、叔齐吧!"又讲到柳下惠、少连,说:"降低自己的志气,辱没

自己的身份,但说话合乎法度,行为经过考虑,不过就是这样罢了。"谈到虞仲、夷逸,说:"逃世隐居,放胆直言。自身清廉,被废弃也合乎权宜。我则和他们不一样,没有什么可以,也没有什么不可以。"

The men who had retired to privacy from the world were Boyi, Shuqi, Yuzhong, Yiyi, Zhuzhang, Liuxia Hui and Shaolian. The Master said, "Those who would not bend their will, or bring humiliation upon themselves were Boyi and Shuqi. It may be said of Liuxia Hui and Shaolian, that they bend their wills, and bring humiliation upon themselves, but their words corresponded with moral principles, and their actions were after consideration, this and no more. It may be said of Yuzhong and Yiyi, that they lived in seclusion, but gave the rein to the tongue. They preserved their purity. Their retreat was timely. But I am different from all of them. I know not 'must' or 'must not'."

[原文]

18·9 大师挚适齐,亚饭干适楚,三饭缭适蔡,四饭缺适秦,鼓方叔入于河,播鼗武入于汉,少师阳、击磬襄入于海。

[译文]

太师挚前往齐国,亚饭乐师干前往楚国,三饭乐师缭前往蔡国,四饭乐师缺前往秦国,击鼓乐师方叔入居黄河之滨,摇小鼓乐师武逃居汉水之滨,少师阳和击磬的乐师襄到海边去了。

The grand music-master Zhi went to Qi; Gan, the master of the band at the second meal, went to Chu; Liao, the band-master at the third meal, went to Cai; Que, the band-master at the fourth meal, went to Qin. The drum-master Fangshu went the Yellow River; The hand-drum master Wu, went to the Han River; Yang, the assistant music-master and Xiang, the master of the stonechimes went to an island in the sea.

[原文] **18·10** 周公谓鲁公曰:"君子不施其亲,不使大臣怨乎不以。故旧无大故,则不弃也。无求备于一人。"

[译文] 周公对他儿子鲁公伯禽说:"君子不怠慢他的亲族,不让大臣抱怨未被信任,老臣旧友没有严重过失就不要抛弃他们,对一个人不要求全责备。"

The Duke of Zhou addressed his son the Duke of Lu, saying, "A virtuous prince does not discard his kinsmen, nor does he cause the great minister to repine at not being used. He does not dismiss any old ministers or friends, unless he has good cause. He asks perfection of no man."

[原文] **18·11** 周有八士:伯达、伯适、仲突、仲忽、叔夜、叔夏、季随、季騧。

[译文] 周朝有八位有教养的人:伯达、伯适、仲突、仲忽、叔夜、叔夏、季随、季騧。

Zhou had eight virtuous men (Shi): Boda, Bokuo, Zhongtu, Zhonghu, Shuye, Shuxia, Jisui, and Jigua.

子张篇第十九

[原文] **19·1** 子张曰："士见危致命，见得思义，祭思敬，丧思哀，其可已矣。"

[译文] 子张说："士遇到危险就献出生命，看见有利可图便考虑该得不该得，祭祀时考虑是否严肃认真，有丧事时考虑是否悲痛哀伤，那也就可以了。"

Zizhang said, "The virtuous man(Shi), who on face of danger is ready to sacrifice his life, who in sight of gain thinks first of righteousness, who keeps reverence in heart when sacrificing, who keeps grief in mind when mourning—such a man is all right."

[原文] **19·2** 子张曰："执德不弘，信道不笃，焉能为有？焉能为亡？"

[译文] 子张说："遵守道德不坚决，信仰真理不忠诚，这种人，有他也可，没他也可。"

Zizhang said, "When a man holds fast virtue, but without enlarging it, and believes in the Way, but without firm sincerity, can this kind of man be said to be, or be said not to be?"

[原文] **19·3** 子夏之门人问交于子张。子张曰："子夏云何？"

对曰："子夏曰：'可者与之，其不可者拒之。'"

子张曰："异乎吾所闻：君子尊贤而容众，嘉善而矜不能。我之大贤与，于人何所不容？我之不贤与，人将拒我，如之何其拒人也？”

［译文］ 子夏的学生问子张如何交朋友。子张说：“子夏说了些什么呢？”

子夏的学生回答说：“子夏说：‘可以交便和他交朋友，不可以交的便拒绝他。’”

子张说：“我所听到的和这不同：君子尊敬贤人，而且容纳众人，称赞好人，而且同情无能的人。我是大贤人，对别人有什么不能容纳的呢？我是不贤的人，别人会拒绝我，我怎么能拒绝别人呢？”

The disciples of Zixia asked Zizhang about the principles of association. Zizhang said, “What does Zixia say?”

They replied, “Zixia says, ‘Associate with those who are worthy associating with, and put away from those who are not worth associating.”

Zizhong said, “This is different from what I have learned. A superior man honours the talented and virtuous, and bears with all. He praises the good and pities the incompetent. If I am a man of great talents and virtue, whom could I not bear with? If I am a man without talents and virtue, men will put me away from them. Why should I push others away?”

［原文］ **19·4** 子夏曰：“虽小道，必有可观者焉；致远恐泥，是以君子不为也。”

［译文］ 子夏说：“虽然是小小的技艺，也一定有值得一顾的地方。但恐怕对远大的事业有妨碍，所以君子不去干。”

Zixia said, “Even the minor crafts have something worth being looked at. But they tend to prove a hindrance to lofty ideals. For that reason a superior man does not practise them."

[原文] **19·5** 子夏曰:"日知其所亡,月无忘其所能,可谓好学也已矣。"

[译文] 子夏说:"每天知晓自己所不知道的,每月不忘记已经能够掌握的,可以说是爱好学习了。"

Zixia said, "He who from day to day learns something new, and from month to month does not forget what he has already learnt, may indeed be called fond of learning."

[原文] **19·6** 子夏曰:"博学而笃志,切问而近思,仁在其中矣。"

[译文] 子夏说:"广博地学习,而且志向专一不变;对未曾理解的事恳切地向人求教,而且考虑当前的问题,仁德便在这当中了。"

Zixia said, "He who studies widely and with a firm aim, who inquires with earnestness, and reflects with self application comes to virtue."

[原文] **19·7** 子夏曰:"百工居肆以成其事,君子学以致其道。"

[译文] 子夏说:"各业的工匠在作坊里来完成他们的工作,君子则通过学习来获得真理。"

Zixia said, "The hundred apprentices live in their workshops in order to accomplish their works. A superior man studies in order to reach the Way."

[原文] **19·8 子夏曰:“小人之过也必文。”**

[译文] 子夏说:“小人有了过失,一定加以掩饰。”

Zixia said, “The small men always gloss their faults.”

[原文] **19·9 子夏曰:“君子有三变:望之俨然,即之也温,听其言也厉。”**

[译文] 子夏说:“对君子的印象有三种变化:远远望去,庄严可畏;向他接近,温和可亲;听他的话,严厉不苟。”

Zixia said, “A superior man undergoes three changes. Seen from afar he looks stern; when approached, he is mild; when heard speaking, he is incisive.”

[原文] **19·10 子夏曰:“君子信而后劳其民;未信,则以为厉己也。信而后谏;未信,则以为谤己也。”**

[译文] 子夏说:“君子必须得到信任以后才去使唤百姓;没有得到信任,他们会认为你在折磨他们;得到信任才去规劝上级;没有得到信任,上级会认为你在毁谤他。”

Zixia said, “A superior man will not lay burdens on the people unless he has gained their trust, otherwise the people will think that he is oppressing them. He will not remonstrate with his prince unless he has gained his trust, otherwise the prince will think that he is slandering him.”

[原文] **19·11 子夏曰:“大德不逾闲,小德出入可也。”**

[译文] 子夏说:“在重大节操上不能超越界限,生活小节上稍有出入是可以的。”

Zixia said, “One must not transgress the boundary-line in

the main principles, but he may pass or repass it in the small trifles."

[原文] 19·12 子游曰:"子夏之门人小子,当洒扫应对进退,则可矣,抑末也。本之则无,如之何?"

子夏闻之,曰:"噫!言游过矣!君子之道,孰先传焉?孰后倦焉?譬诸草木,区以别矣。君子之道,焉可诬也?有始有卒者,其惟圣人乎!"

[译文] 子游说:"子夏的学生们做做洒水扫地、接待客人、应对进退的事情,那是可以的,但这些只是末节小事。在学术上他们却没有基础,这怎么行呢?"

子夏听到了,说:"唉!言游错了!君子的学术哪些先传授,哪些后讲述呢?譬如草木,各种各类是应该区别开来,君子的学术,怎么可以歪曲呢?传授学术有始有终的,大概只有圣人吧!"

Ziyou said, "The disciples of Zixia, in sprinkling and sweeping floors, in answering and replying, in advancing and receding, are all right. But these are minor matters. They are left ignorant of what is essential. But what can come of branches without root?"

When Zixia heard of this, he said, "Alas, Yan You is wrong. Of the ways of the superior man, which is to be delivered first, and which is to be idled about? As in the case of plants, they have to be separately treated according to their classes. How can the ways of a superior man be misrepresented? It is the sage alone who can transmit knowledge from beginning to end!"

[原文] **19·13** 子夏曰:“仕而优则学,学而优则仕。”

[译文] 子夏说:“官做好了,有余力就学习;学习好了,有余力就去做官。”

Zixia said, “The officer, after doing all his duty to the state, should devote his spare energy to study. The scholar, after completing his studying, should devote his spare energy to service of the state.”

[原文] **19·14** 子游曰:“丧致乎哀而止。”

[译文] 子游说:“居丧时,充分表现了他心中的悲哀也就够了。”

Ziyou said, “Mourning, having been carried to the utmost degree of grief, should go no further.”

[原文] **19·15** 子游曰:“吾友张也为难能也,然而未仁。”

[译文] 子游说:“我的朋友子张是难能可贵的,但还没有做到仁。”

Ziyou said, “My friend Zizhang can do things that are hard to be done, but yet he is not perfectly virtuous (Ren).”

[原文] **19·16** 曾子曰:“堂堂乎张也,难与并为仁矣。”

[译文] 曾子说:“子张的为人高不可攀,很难把别人一同带入仁德的境界。”

Zeng Zi said, “How imposing is the manner of Zizang! It is difficult with him to practise perfect virtue.”

[原文] **19·17** 曾子曰:“吾闻诸夫子:人未有自致者也,必也亲丧乎!”

［译文］ 曾子说:“我听老师说过,人没有把内心的真实感情表露出来的时候,如果有,一定在父母逝世的时候吧!”

Zeng Zi said, “I once heard the Master said that men may not show what is in them to the full extent, and yet they will be found to do so when mourning for their parents.”

［原文］ **19·18 曾子曰:“吾闻诸夫子:孟庄子之孝也,其他可能也;其不改父之臣与父之政,是难能也。”**

［译文］ 曾子说:“我听老师说过:孟庄子的孝道,其他都可以做到。而他在职期间,留用他父亲的僚属,保持他父亲的政治措施,这是不容易做到的。”

Zeng Zi said, “I once heard the Master said that in all else we may rival the filial piety of Meng Zhuang Zi, but in his not changing his father's ministers, nor his father's mode of government, he is hard to rival.”

［原文］ **19·19 孟氏使阳肤为士师,问于曾子。曾子曰:“上失其道,民散久矣。如得其情,则哀矜而勿喜!”**

［译文］ 孟氏任命阳肤做法官,阳肤向曾子求教。曾子说:“在上位的人不依规矩行事,百姓的心早就涣散了。你如果能审出罪犯的真情,就应该可怜、同情他们,不要自鸣得意。”

The chief of the Meng family appointed Yang Fu① as chief criminal judge. Yang Fu consulted Zeng Zi. Zeng Zi said, “The rulers have failed in their duties, and the people have gone astray for a long time. When you have found out the truth of any crime, be sad and pity them, and do not feel joyful.”

[注释] ① A disciple of Zeng Zi.

[原文] **19·20** 子贡曰："纣之不善，不如是之甚也。是以君子恶居下流，天下之恶皆归焉。"

[译文] 子贡说："商纣王的罪恶，不像传说的那么厉害。所以君子最怕沾着恶名，一沾恶名，天下什么坏事都会集中在他身上。"

Zigong said, "The wickedness of King Zhou was not as great as that name implies. Therefore, a superior man hates to dwell on low ground, where all the evil of the world will flow in upon him."

[原文] **19·21** 子贡曰："君子之过也，如日月之食焉：过也，人皆见之；更也，人皆仰之。"

[译文] 子贡说："君子的过失如同日蚀月蚀一样：犯错误的时候，人人都能看得见；当改正的时候，人人都仰望着。"

Zigong said, "The faults of a superior man are like the eclipses of the sun and the moon. When he has his faults, all men see them; when he corrects his faults, all men look up to him."

[原文] **19·22** 卫公孙朝问于子贡曰："仲尼焉学？"子贡曰："文武之道，未坠于地，在人。贤者识其大者，不贤者识其小者。莫不有文武之道焉。夫子焉不学？而亦何常师之有？"

[译文] 卫国的公孙朝问子贡说："仲尼的学问是从哪里得来的？"子贡说："周文王、武王的道术并没有失传，散在人间。贤能的人抓住大节，不贤能的人只抓住小节。没有地方没有文王、武王的道术。我的老师到哪里不能学呢？又为什么一定要有专门的老师传授呢？"

Gongsun Chao of Wei asked Zigong, "Where did Zhongni get his learning?" Zigong said, "The Way of King Wen and King Wu of Zhou have not fallen into ruin. They are to be found among men. Men of talents and virtue grasp the major principles of them, and men without such talents and virtue grasp the minor principles. So there is no one who does not possess the Way of Wen and Wu. From whom indeed did our Master not learn? What need had he for a fixed teacher?"

[原文] **19·23** 叔孙武叔语大夫于朝曰:"子贡贤于仲尼。"

子服景伯以告子贡。

子贡曰:"譬之宫墙,赐之墙也及肩,窥见室家之好。夫子之墙数仞,不得其门而入,不见宗庙之美,百官之富。得其门者或寡矣。夫子之云,不亦宜乎!"

[译文] 叔孙武叔在朝廷告诉大夫们说:"子贡比他老师仲尼还要好。"

子服景伯把这话告诉了子贡。

子贡说:"拿房屋的围墙作比喻吧,我家的围墙只齐肩膀,谁都可以望见房屋的美好。我老师的围墙有几丈高,人们找不着大门进去,就看不到他那宗庙的壮美,房舍的多种多样。能够找着大门进去的人或许不多吧。叔孙武叔他老人家那么说,不也是很自然的吗?"

Shusun Wushu①, talking to some high officers at court, said, "Zigong is better than his master."

Zifu Jingbo told this to Zigong.

Zigong said, "Let me take as the comparison the wall round a house. My wall only reaches to the shoulders. One may peep over it, and see the goodly home within. The Master's wall is several fathoms high. If one does not find the door and enter by it, he cannot see the beauty of the ancestral temple, nor the rich variety of houses. But I think that those who find the door are few. So it is small wonder that he should have spoken like that."

[注释] ① A high official of Lu.

[原文] **19·24** 叔孙武叔毁仲尼。子贡曰:"无以为也!仲尼不可毁也。他人之贤者,丘陵也,犹可逾也;仲尼,日月也,无得而逾焉。人虽欲自绝,其何伤于日月乎?多见其不知量也。"

[译文] 叔孙武叔毁谤仲尼。子贡说:"不要这样做!仲尼是毁谤不了的。别人的贤能好比小山,还可以超过;仲尼好比太阳和月亮一样,是不能超过的。有人纵然想自绝于太阳、月亮,那对太阳、月亮又有什么损害呢?只是看出他太不自量了。"

Shusun Wushu decried Zhongni. Zigong said, "Don't do that. Zhongni cannot be decried. The talents and virtue of other men are like hillocks and mounds that can be overleaped. Zhongni is like the sun or the moon that it is impossible to step over. If a man cut himself from them, what harm can he do to the sun or the moon? It only shows that he does not know his own measure."

[原文] **19·25** 陈子禽谓子贡曰:"子为恭也,仲尼岂贤于子乎?"

子贡曰:"君子一言以为知,一言以为不知,言不可不慎也。夫子之不可及也,犹天之不可阶而升也。夫子之得邦家者,所谓立之斯立,道之斯行,绥之斯来,动之斯和。其生也荣,其死也哀,如之何其可及也?"

[译文] 陈子禽对子贡说:"您对仲尼那么恭敬,难道他比您强吗?"

子贡说:"君子说一句话可以表现他的聪明,也可以说一句话表现他不聪明,说话是不能不谨慎的。我的老师是不可赶上的,如同上天不能用梯子一级级地爬上去一样。我的老师如果当上国家的君主,或得到采邑成为卿大夫,他要百姓在社会上站住脚跟,百姓便都自然站住脚跟;引导百姓前进,百姓自然都跟着前进;安抚百姓,百姓自然都会前来投奔;动员百姓,百姓自然会同心协力。他老人家生得光荣,死得可惜可悲,别人怎么能赶得上呢?"

Chen Ziqin said to Zigong, "You are too modest. How can Zhongni be said to be superior to you?"

Zigong said, "For one word a superior man may be set down as wise, and for one word he is deemed to be not wise. So we should be careful indeed about what we say. None can equal the Master, as heaven cannot be climbed up to by a ladder. Had the master ever been put in control of a state or of a great family, it would have been as is described in the words: —He raised them and they stand; he leads them on and they follow; he pacifies them and they come up to him; he stimulates them and they are harmonious. His life was glorious, his death was bitterly lamented. How can he ever be equalled?"

尧曰篇第二十

[原文] **20·1** 尧曰："咨！尔舜！天之历数在尔躬，允执其中。四海困穷，天禄永终。"

舜亦以命禹。

[译文] 尧（禅位给舜的时候）说："啧啧！你这位舜呀！上天的大任已经落到你身上了，你要真诚地坚持正确的方针。如果天下的百姓都陷入困苦贫穷的境地，上天给你的禄位也就会永远终止了。"

舜（禅位时），也这样告诫禹。

[原文] 曰："予小子履敢用玄牡，敢昭告于皇皇后帝：有罪不敢赦。帝臣不蔽，简在帝心。朕躬有罪，无以万方；万方有罪，罪在朕躬。"

[译文] （商汤时，遭逢大旱，汤向上天求雨，）说："我这小子履谨用黑色的牡牛作祭品，明白地禀告辉煌的天帝：有罪的人不敢赦免他。您臣仆的善恶我也不掩盖，您心里是晓得的。我本人有罪，不要牵连天下万方；天下万方有罪，都归罪我一人。"

[原文] 周有大赉，善人是富。"虽有周亲，不如仁人。百姓有过，在予一人。"

[译文] 周朝大加封赏，使善良的人都富贵起来。周武王说："我虽然有至亲，不如有仁德之人。百姓有过错，由我一人来承担。"

[原文] 谨权量，审法度，修废官，四方之政行焉。兴灭国，继绝世，举逸民，天下之民归心焉。

[译文] 谨慎地检查度量衡，审订礼乐制度，恢复已废弃的官职，

全国政令就会通行了。恢复被灭亡的国家,接续已断绝的世族,选拔被遗落的人才,天下的百姓就都会心悦诚服。

[原文] **所重:民、食、丧、祭。**

[译文] 所重视的是:百姓、粮食、丧礼、祭祀。

[原文] **宽则得众,信则民任焉,敏则有功,公则说。**

[译文] 宽厚就会得到众人的拥护,诚信就会得到别人的任用,勤快就会有功绩,公平就会使百姓高兴。

Yao said, "Oh! you, Shun, the heavenly order of succession now rest in your own person. Faithfully hold fast the golden mean. If there shall be distress and want within the four seas, your heavenly gift will pass for ever."

Shun also said the same words in giving his charge to Yu.

Tang① said, "I, your child Lü, venture to sacrifice a black ox, and venture to proclaim before you, O most great and sovereign God, that I dare not forgive the sinner, nor slay your servants. Oh God, you know all about this. If I in my person do any wrong, let it never be visited on the people of myriad regions. If in the myriad regions any wrong be done, let it be visited upon my person."

Zhou granted titles and territories, and the good were enriched. King Wu said, "Although I have my own kinsmen, they are less to me than the virtuous. If the people do wrong, let the blame be thrown upon me alone."

Attend to weights and measures, revise the system ritual, restore the discarded offices, thus order will reign on all sides. Revive states that had been destroyed, re-establish lines of succession that had been broken, and call to office those who had been neglected, then all hearts of the people under Heaven will turn to him.

What the greatest attention should be paid to were the people, the food, the rites of mourning and sacrifice.

Generosity wins all; sincerity wins the people's trust; diligence brings the success; and justice delights all.

[注释]

① Founder of the Yin dynasty, when praying Heaven for rain.

[原文]

20·2 子张问于孔子曰:"何如斯可以从政矣?"

子曰:"尊五美,屏四恶,斯可以从政矣。"

子张曰:"何谓五美?"

子曰:"君子惠而不费,劳而不怨,欲而不贪,泰而不骄,威而不猛。"

子张曰:"何谓惠而不费?"

子曰:"因民之所利而利之,斯不亦惠而不费乎?择可劳而劳之,又谁怨?欲仁而得仁,又焉贪?君子无众寡,无小大,无敢慢,斯不亦泰而不骄乎?君子正其衣冠,尊其瞻视,俨然人望而畏之,斯不亦威而不猛乎?"

子张曰:"何谓四恶?"

子曰:"不教而杀谓之虐;不戒视成谓之暴;慢令致期谓之贼;犹之与人也,出纳之吝谓之有司。"

[译文]

子张问孔子说:"怎样才可以治理政事呢?"

孔子说:"尊崇五种美德,排除四种恶政,这就可以治理政事了。"

子张说:"什么是五种美德?"

孔子说:"君子给人民好处,自己却不耗费;使唤百姓,百姓却不怨恨；自己有所求，却不贪婪；安宁矜持却不骄傲；有威严却不凶猛。”

子张说：“什么是给人民好处，而自己却不耗费？”

孔子说：“凡百姓能得到好处的便使他们得到好处；这不就是给人民好处，自己却不耗费吗？选择可以劳动的（时间、地点和对象）再去叫他们劳动，又有谁会怨恨呢？自己想要仁德便得到仁德，还贪求什么呢？无论人多人少，无论势力大小，君子都不敢怠慢，这不是矜持安宁而不骄傲吗？君子衣冠整齐，目不邪视，态度庄重，使人望见有所畏惧，这不是有威严却不凶猛吗？”

子张说：“四种恶政又是什么呢？”

孔子说：“不先教育便加杀戮叫做虐；不先告诫便求有成绩叫做暴；下达可以缓慢执行的命令，而突然要求限期完成叫做贼；同是给人财物，出手吝啬，叫做小气。”

Zizhang asked Confucius, “What must a man do that he may conduct government properly?”

The Master said, “He, who esteems the five virtues, and avoid the four vices, may conduct government properly.”

Zizhang said, “What are the five virtues?”

The Master said, “A superior man is benevolent without great expenditure; he lays tasks on the people without arousing their resentment; he has desires without being covetous; he maintains a dignified ease without being proud; he inspires awe without being fierce.”

Zizhang said, “What is meant by being benevolent without great expenditure?”

The Master said, “If he makes more beneficial to the people the things from which they naturally derive benefit, is he not benevolent without great expenditure? If he imposes upon them only such tasks as they are capable of performing, is he not laying tasks on them without arousing their resentment? If his desires are set on human-heartedness and he gets it, who can say that he is covetous? Whether a superior man has to deal many people or few, or with things great or small, he dares not slight them: is not this maintaining, a dignified ease without any pride? A superior man straightens his robe and hat, and imparts a dignity into his looks, so that, thus dignified, men look up to him with awe: is not this inspiring awe without fierce?"

Zizhang asked, "What are the four vices?"

The Master said, "To put the people to death without having instructed them, this is called cruelty. To require from them the completion of tasks without giving them due warning, this is called oppression. To give careless orders, and be strict when the day comes, this is called robbery. And to be stingy in paying or rewarding men is called littleness."

[原文] **20·3** 孔子曰:"不知命,无以为君子也;不知礼,无以立也;不知言,无以知人也。"

[译文] 孔子说:"不懂得命运,没有办法做君子;不懂得礼节,没有办法立足于社会;不善于分析人家的言论,没办法了解人。"

Confucius said, "He who does not know the will of Heaven cannot be regarded as a superior man. He who does not know the rules of propriety cannot take his stand. He who does not know words cannot know people."

图书在版编目(CIP)数据

论语今译:汉、英／杨伯峻,吴树平等今译. —济南:齐鲁书社,2009.4 (2014.11 重印)
(齐鲁文化经典文库)
ISBN 978-7-5333-2162-8

Ⅰ. 论… Ⅱ. 杨… Ⅲ. ①儒家②论语—译文—汉、英 Ⅳ. B222.24

中国版本图书馆 CIP 数据核字(2009)第 016948 号

齐鲁文化经典文库
论语今译
杨伯峻 吴树平 今译
潘富恩 温少霞 英译

主管单位	山东出版传媒股份有限公司
出版发行	齊魯書社
社　　址	济南市英雄山路 189 号
邮　　编	250002
网　　址	www.qlss.com.cn
电子邮箱	qilupress@126.com
营销中心	(0531)82098521　82098519
印　　刷	山东临沂新华印刷物流集团有限责任公司
开　　本	720mm×1020mm　1/16
印　　张	15.75
插　　页	3
字　　数	219 千
版　　次	2009 年 4 月第 1 版
印　　次	2014 年 11 月第 3 次印刷
标准书号	ISBN 978-7-5333-2162-8
定　　价	**30.00 元**